CONTENTS

ENJOY YOUR AIR FRYER

Do you love fried foods but try to avoid them? You no longer need to worry.

The air fryer is your answer to preparing fried foods without the extra calories, fat, or mess in the kitchen. You'll get the taste and texture of fried foods—crispy, tasty, and crunchy—that you love and crave, without the added guilt often felt when consuming them. Plus, you'll soon see how your air fryer is so easy to use, cooks food faster, and provides a no-fuss clean up.

You'll love the ability to prepare fried foods in your air fryer, but you'll also soon find that you can prepare all types of other foods, too. Make everything from appetizers to meals to sides and even desserts! You can bake in it, grill in it, steam in it, roast in it, and reheat in it.

Choose from more than 120 ideas here, or create your own.

Now get started and have fun eating and serving all those healthier foods without the added guilt.

HELPFUL HINTS

- Read the air fryer's manufacturer's directions carefully before cooking to make sure you understand the specific features of your air fryer before starting to cook.

- Preheat your air fryer for 2 to 3 minutes before cooking.

- You can cook foods typically cooked in the oven in your air fryer. But because the air fryer is more condensed than a regular oven, it is recommended that recipes cut 25°F to 50°F off the temperature and 20% off the typical cooking times.

- Avoid having foods stick to your air fryer basket by using nonstick cooking spray or cooking on parchment paper or foil. You can also get food to brown and crisp more easily by spraying occasionally with nonstick cooking spray during the cooking process.

- Don't overfill your basket. Each air fryer differs in its basket size. Cook foods in batches as needed.

- Use toothpicks to hold food in place. You may notice that light foods may blow around from the pressure of the fan. Just be sure to secure foods in the basket to prevent this.

- Check foods while cooking by opening the air fryer basket. This will not disturb cooking times. Once you return the basket, the cooking resumes.

- Experiment with cooking times of various foods. Test foods for doneness before consuming—check meats and poultry with a meat thermometer, and use a toothpick to test muffins and cupcakes.

- Use your air fryer to cook frozen foods, too! Frozen French fries, fish sticks, chicken nuggets, individual pizzas—these all work great. Just remember to reduce cooking temperatures and times.

ESTIMATED COOKING TEMPERATURES/TIMES*

FOOD	TEMPERATURE	TIMING
Vegetables (asparagus, broccoli, corn-on-cob, green beans, mushrooms, cherry tomatoes)	390°F	5 to 6 min.
Vegetables (bell peppers, cauliflower, eggplant, onions, potatoes, zucchini)	390°F	8 to 12 min.
Chicken (bone-in)	370°F	20 to 25 min.
Chicken (boneless)	370°F	12 to 15 min.
Beef (ground beef)	370°F	15 to 17 min.
Beef (steaks, roasts)	390°F	10 to 15 min.
Pork	370°F	12 to 15 min.
Fish	390°F	10 to 12 min.
Frozen Foods	390°F	10 to 15 min.

This is just a guide. All food varies in size, weight, and texture. Be sure to test your food for preferred doneness before consuming it. Also, some foods will need to be shaken or flipped to help distribute ingredients for proper cooking.

Make note of the temperatures and times that work best for you for continued success of your air fryer.

Enjoy and have fun!

START OFF YOUR DAY

AIR-FRIED OMELET SCRAMBLE

2 **large eggs**

2 **tablespoons milk**

¼ **teaspoon salt**

⅛ **teaspoon black pepper**

2 **tablespoons chopped red and/ or green bell pepper**

2 **tablespoons chopped onion**

¼ **cup (1 ounce) shredded Cheddar cheese, divided**

1 Spray 6×3-inch baking dish or 2 small ramekins* with nonstick cooking spray.

2 Whisk eggs, milk, salt and black pepper in medium bowl. Add bell pepper, onion and 2 tablespoons cheese. Pour into prepared dish.

3 Preheat air fryer to 350°F. Cook 10 to 12 minutes slightly breaking up eggs after 5 minutes. Top with remaining cheese.

Depending on the size of your air fryer, you may need to modify the size of the baking dish.

MAKES 2 SERVINGS

CALORIES 110 · TOTAL FAT 7g · SATURATED FAT 3.5g · CHOLESTEROL 110mg
SODIUM 430mg · CARBOHYDRATE 3g · DIETARY FIBER 0g · PROTEIN 7g

AIR-FRIED HARD COOKED EGGS

1 to 6 eggs

1 Preheat air fryer to 270°F.

2 Carefully place eggs in basket. Cook 15 minutes.

3 Remove eggs; place in cold water to cool.

MAKE AS DESIRED (NUTRITION INFORMATION FOR 1 EGG)

CALORIES 80 · TOTAL FAT 5g · SATURATED FAT 1.5g · CHOLESTEROL 185mg
SODIUM 60mg · CARBOHYDRATE 1g · DIETARY FIBER 0g · PROTEIN 6g

QUICK JELLY-FILLED BISCUIT DOUGHNUT BALLS

1 **package (about 7 ounces) refrigerated reduced-fat biscuit dough (10 biscuits)**

¼ **cup coarse sugar**

1 **cup strawberry preserves***

*If preserves are very chunky, process in food processor 10 seconds or press through fine-mesh sieve.

1 Preheat air fryer to 370°F.

2 Separate biscuits into 10 portions. Cut each in half; roll dough into balls to create 20 balls.

3 Cook in batches 5 to 6 minutes or until golden brown.

4 Place sugar in large bowl. Coat warm balls in sugar. Let cool. Using a piping bag with medium star tip; fill bag with preserves. Poke hole in side of each doughnut ball with paring knife; fill with preserves. Serve immediately.

MAKES 20 DOUGHNUT BALLS

CALORIES 80 · TOTAL FAT 1g · SATURATED FAT 0g · CHOLESTEROL 0mg
SODIUM 80mg · CARBOHYDRATE 17g · DIETARY FIBER 0g · PROTEIN 1g

HOMEMADE AIR-FRIED BAGELS

1 cup self-rising flour

1 cup plain nonfat Greek yogurt

1 large egg, beaten

Sesame seeds, poppy seeds, dried onion flakes, everything bagel seasoning (optional)

Cream cheese or butter (optional)

1   Combine flour and yogurt in bowl of electric stand mixer with dough hook*. Beat 2 to 3 minutes or until mixture is well combined. Place dough on lightly floured surface; knead by hand about 4 to 5 minutes or until dough is smooth and elastic. Form dough into a ball.

2   Cut into 4 equal portions. Roll each into a ball. Pull and stretch dough to create desired shape, inserting finger into center to create hole. Repeat with remaining dough.

3   Preheat air fryer to 330°F. Line basket with parchment paper. Place bagels on parchment; brush with egg wash. Sprinkle with desired toppings. Cook 8 to 10 minutes or until lightly browned.

4   Serve with cream cheese or butter, if desired.

Or, use heavy spatula in large bowl to combine mixture.

MAKES 4 SERVINGS

CALORIES 150 · TOTAL FAT 1g · SATURATED FAT 0g · CHOLESTEROL 50mg
SODIUM 440mg · CARBOHYDRATE 25g · DIETARY FIBER 1g · PROTEIN 10g

CAULIFLOWER "HASH BROWN" PATTIES

4 slices bacon

1 package (about 12 ounces) cauliflower rice

½ cup finely chopped onion

½ cup finely chopped red and/or green bell pepper

1 large egg

⅓ cup all-purpose flour

½ cup (2 ounces) shredded Cheddar cheese

1 tablespoon chopped fresh chives

1 teaspoon salt

½ teaspoon black pepper

1 Preheat air fryer to 400°F. Cook bacon 8 to 10 minutes. Remove from basket to paper towels; blot any grease from bacon. Crumble into small pieces.

2 Place cauliflower in large bowl. Add bacon, onion, bell pepper, egg, flour, cheese, chives, salt and black pepper; mix well. Shape mixture into patties; place on baking sheet. Freeze 30 minutes.

3 Preheat air fryer to 370°F. Spray basket with nonstick cooking spray. Cook 12 to 15 minutes or until browned.

MAKES 8 SERVINGS

CALORIES 90 · TOTAL FAT 4g · SATURATED FAT 2g · CHOLESTEROL 35mg
SODIUM 480mg · CARBOHYDRATE 8g · DIETARY FIBER 1g · PROTEIN 6g

BEDROCK FRUIT BOULDERS

1¼ **cups finely chopped apple (1 small apple)**

⅓ **cup dried mixed fruit bits**

2 **tablespoons packed brown sugar**

½ **teaspoon ground cinnamon**

1 **package (about 16 ounces) refrigerated jumbo buttermilk biscuit dough (8 biscuits)**

1 **cup powdered sugar**

4 **to 5 teaspoons orange juice**

1 Combine apple, dried fruit, brown sugar and cinnamon in small bowl; mix well.

2 Separate biscuits; cut each biscuit in half horizontally to create 16 rounds. Roll each round into 3½-inch circle. Spoon 1 rounded tablespoon apple mixture into center of each circle. Moisten edges of dough with water. Pull dough up and around filling, completely enclosing filling. Pinch edges to seal.

3 Preheat air fryer to 330°F. Line basket with parchment paper; spray with nonstick cooking spray. Place biscuits, seam side down, in basket.

4 Cook in batches 10 to 12 minutes or until golden brown. Remove to wire rack; cool 10 minutes.

5 Combine powdered sugar and 4 teaspoons orange juice in small bowl; whisk until smooth. Add additional orange juice, if necessary, to reach drizzling consistency. Spoon glaze over rolls. Serve warm.

MAKES 16 SERVINGS

CALORIES 140 · TOTAL FAT 3.5g · SATURATED FAT 2g · CHOLESTEROL 0mg
SODIUM 270mg · CARBOHYDRATE 26g · DIETARY FIBER 0g · PROTEIN 2g

BREAKFAST FLATS

1 **package (about 14 ounces) refrigerated pizza dough**

1½ **cups (6 ounces) shredded Cheddar cheese**

8 **slices bacon, crisp-cooked and diced (optional)**

4 **eggs, fried**

Kosher salt and black pepper (optional)

1 Divide pizza dough into 4 equal portions. Roll out on lightly floured surface into rectangles roughly 8½×4 inches. Top each evenly with cheese and bacon, if desired.

2 Preheat air fryer to 370°F. Line basket with parchment paper.

3 Cook in batches 5 to 7 minutes or until crust is golden brown and crisp and cheese is melted.

4 Top baked flats with fried egg; season with salt and pepper, if desired. Serve warm.

MAKES 4 SERVINGS

CALORIES 290 · TOTAL FAT 11g · SATURATED FAT 5g · CHOLESTEROL 200mg
SODIUM 630mg · CARBOHYDRATE 32g · DIETARY FIBER 0g · PROTEIN 14g

WHOLE GRAIN FRENCH TOAST

½ **cup egg substitute *or* 2 egg whites**

¼ **cup low-fat (1%) milk**

½ **teaspoon ground cinnamon**

¼ **teaspoon ground nutmeg**

4 **teaspoons butter**

8 **slices 100% whole wheat or multigrain bread**

⅓ **cup pure maple syrup**

1 **cup fresh blueberries**

2 **teaspoons powdered sugar**

1 Preheat air fryer to 370°F. Spray basket with nonstick cooking spray.

2 Whisk egg substitute, milk, cinnamon and nutmeg in shallow bowl until well blended. Melt 1 teaspoon butter in large nonstick skillet over medium heat. Working with 2 slices at a time, dip each bread slice in milk mixture, turning to coat both sides; let excess mixture drip back into bowl.

3 Cook in batches 5 to 7 minutes or until golden brown, flipping halfway during cooking.

4 Microwave maple syrup in small microwavable bowl on HIGH 30 seconds or until bubbly. Stir in blueberries. Serve French toast with blueberry mixture; sprinkle with powdered sugar.

MAKES 4 SERVINGS (2 SLICES FRENCH TOAST AND ¼ CUP BLUEBERRY MIXTURE PER SERVING)

CALORIES 251 · TOTAL FAT 6g · SATURATED FAT 3g · CHOLESTEROL 11mg · SODIUM 324mg · CARBOHYDRATE 46g · DIETARY FIBER 5g · PROTEIN 12g

BROILED GRAPEFRUIT YOUR WAY

1 **large pink grapefruit**

2 **teaspoons honey**

2 **teaspoons packed brown sugar**

1 Cut grapefruit in half horizontally. Use a sharp knife to cut around edges and sections of grapefruit where the rind meets the fruit.

2 Drizzle each half with honey; sprinkle with brown sugar.

3 Preheat air fryer to 400°F. Cook 5 to 7 minutes until lightly browned and bubbly.

MAKES 2 SERVINGS

VARIATION: Sprinkle grapefruit with cinnamon-sugar mixture or toasted coconut instead of honey and brown sugar.

CALORIES 80 · TOTAL FAT 0g · SATURATED FAT 0g · CHOLESTEROL 0mg
SODIUM 0mg · CARBOHYDRATE 19g · DIETARY FIBER 1g · PROTEIN 1g

BREAKFAST BURRITOS

4 turkey breakfast sausage links

2 eggs

½ teaspoon ground cumin (optional)

4 (6-inch) yellow or white corn tortillas

¼ cup salsa

1   Preheat air fryer to 370°F. Line basket with parchment paper.

2   Cook sausages 6 to 8 minutes or until browned on the outside and cooked through, shaking occasionally during cooking. Remove to plate.

3   Whisk eggs and cumin, if desired, in small bowl. Heat small skillet over medium-high heat. Cook eggs until done.

4   Place sausage link in middle of each tortilla. Spoon equal amounts of scrambled egg on top of sausage. Roll up to enclose the filling; secure with toothpicks.

5   Cook in air fryer 2 to 3 minutes or until heated through.

6   Pour salsa in small bowl. Serve with burritos.

MAKES 4 SERVINGS

CALORIES 130 · TOTAL FAT 5g · SATURATED FAT 1.5g · CHOLESTEROL 110mg
SODIUM 310mg · CARBOHYDRATE 12g · DIETARY FIBER 0g · PROTEIN 8g

FRENCH TOAST STICKS

4 **eggs**

⅓ **cup reduced-fat (2%) milk**

1 **teaspoon ground cinnamon**

1 **teaspoon vanilla**

4 **slices Italian bread, cut into 3 portions each**

1 **teaspoon powdered sugar**

¼ **cup maple syrup**

1 Combine eggs, milk, cinnamon and vanilla in large shallow dish.

2 Dip bread sticks in egg mixture to coat.

3 Preheat air fryer to 370°F. Line basket with parchment paper; spray with nonstick cooking spray.

4 Cook in batches 8 to 10 minutes or until golden brown. Dust lightly with powdered sugar; serve with maple syrup.

MAKES 4 SERVINGS

CALORIES 230 · TOTAL FAT 6g · SATURATED FAT 2g · CHOLESTEROL 190mg
SODIUM 250mg · CARBOHYDRATE 31g · DIETARY FIBER 0g · PROTEIN 10g

BISCUIT BREAKFAST PIZZAS

1 package (about 16 ounces) refrigerated flaky biscuit dough

8 tablespoons tomato sauce

2 slices turkey bacon

¼ cup chopped green bell pepper (optional)

¼ cup chopped onion (optional)

1¼ cups egg substitute

¼ teaspoon black pepper

½ cup (2 ounces) shredded Cheddar cheese

1 Separate biscuits. Make indentation in center of each biscuit. Spoon 1 tablespoon tomato sauce into center.

2 Cook bacon, bell pepper and onion, if desired, in large nonstick skillet over medium-high heat until crisp. Remove bacon to paper towels. Drain drippings from skillet.

3 Spray same skillet with nonstick cooking spray. Add egg substitute; season with black pepper. Cook about 1 minute, stirring often, until eggs are set.

4 Spoon eggs evenly into biscuit centers. Crumble bacon; sprinkle over eggs. Top with cheese.

5 Preheat air fryer to 370°F. Cook in batches 6 to 8 minutes or until pizza edges are golden brown.

MAKES 8 SERVINGS

VARIATION: Try substituting low-fat sausage for the bacon in this recipe. Or, try another of your favorite reduced-fat cheeses in place of the Cheddar.

CALORIES 222 · TOTAL FAT 10g · SATURATED FAT 2g · CHOLESTEROL 4mg
SODIUM 812mg · CARBOHYDRATE 25g · DIETARY FIBER 1g · PROTEIN 10g

CHEESE & SAUSAGE BUNDLES

¼ **pound bulk hot Italian pork sausage**

1 **cup (4 ounces) shredded Monterey Jack cheese**

1 **can (4 ounces) diced mild green chiles, drained**

2 **tablespoons finely chopped green onion**

40 **wonton wrappers**

Prepared salsa

1 Brown sausage in small skillet over medium-high heat 6 to 8 minutes, stirring to break up meat. Drain off drippings.

2 Combine sausage, cheese, chiles and green onion in medium bowl. Spoon 1 round teaspoon sausage mixture near one corner of wonton wrapper. Brush opposite corner with water. Fold corner over filling; roll into cylinder.

3 Moisten ends of roll with water. Bring ends together to make a "bundle," overlapping ends slightly; firmly press to seal. Repeat with remaining filling and wonton wrappers.

4 Preheat air fryer to 370°F. Cook in batches 3 to 5 minutes or until golden brown. Serve with salsa.

MAKES 40 BUNDLES

CALORIES 35 · TOTAL FAT 1.5g · SATURATED FAT 1g · CHOLESTEROL 5mg
SODIUM 90mg · CARBOHYDRATE 3g · DIETARY FIBER 0g · PROTEIN 2g

BREAKFAST PEPPERONI FLATBREAD

1 flatbread

½ cup (2 ounces) shredded mozzarella cheese

1 plum tomato, diced

12 slices turkey pepperoni, cut into quarters

1 teaspoon grated Parmesan cheese

¼ cup chopped fresh basil

1 Preheat air fryer to 370°F.

2 Place flatbread on parchment paper. Sprinkle with mozzarella cheese, tomatoes, pepperoni and Parmesan cheese.

3 Cook 3 to 5 minutes or until cheese is melted. Sprinkle with basil. Cool slightly before cutting.

MAKES 2 SERVINGS

CALORIES 170 · TOTAL FAT 8g · SATURATED FAT 4g · CHOLESTEROL 35mg
SODIUM 560mg · CARBOHYDRATE 10g · DIETARY FIBER 0g · PROTEIN 15g

RASPBERRY PUFFS

1 package (8 ounces) refrigerated crescent roll dough

¼ cup raspberry fruit spread

½ of an 8-ounce package cream cheese, softened

1 to 2 teaspoons sugar

2 tablespoons reduced-fat (2%) milk

¼ teaspoon vanilla

1 Separate crescent roll dough into 8 triangles; unroll on lightly floured surface. Brush 1½ teaspoons fruit spread evenly over each roll. Roll up each triangle, starting at wide end.

2 Preheat air fryer to 370°F. Line basket with parchment paper.

3 Cook in batches 5 to 6 minutes or until lightly golden. Cool.

4 Meanwhile, whisk together cream cheese, sugar, milk and vanilla in small bowl until smooth. Spoon about 1 tablespoon cream cheese mixture over each cooled roll or serve on the side, as desired.

MAKES 8 PUFFS

VARIATION: For an even lighter-tasting roll, replace the cream cheese mixture with powdered sugar. Simply sprinkle 2 tablespoons evenly over all.

CALORIES 127 · TOTAL FAT 6g · SATURATED FAT 2g · CHOLESTEROL 6mg
SODIUM 223mg · CARBOHYDRATE 16g · DIETARY FIBER 0g · PROTEIN 3g

APPETIZERS & FINGER FOODS

AIR-FRIED PARMESAN PICKLE CHIPS

- **4 large whole dill pickles**
- **½ cup all-purpose flour**
- **½ teaspoon salt**
- **2 eggs**
- **½ cup panko bread crumbs**
- **2 tablespoons grated Parmesan cheese**
- **½ cup garlic aioli mayonnaise or ranch dressing**

1. Line baking sheet with paper towels. Slice pickles diagonally into ¼-inch slices, place on prepared baking sheet. Pat dry on top with paper towels to remove any moisture from pickles.

2. Combine flour and salt in shallow dish. Beat eggs in another shallow dish. Combine panko and Parmesan cheese in third shallow dish.

3. Coat pickles in flour. Dip in eggs, letting excess drip back into dish, then coat in panko.

4. Preheat air fryer to 390°F. Cook in batches 8 to 10 minutes or until golden brown. Remove carefully. Serve with aioli or dressing.

MAKES 8 SERVINGS

CALORIES 170 • TOTAL FAT 11g • SATURATED FAT 2g • CHOLESTEROL 60mg
SODIUM 880mg • CARBOHYDRATE 12g • DIETARY FIBER 1g • PROTEIN 4g

GREAT ZUKES PIZZA BITES

1 **medium zucchini**

3 **tablespoons pizza sauce**

2 **tablespoons tomato paste**

¼ **teaspoon dried oregano**

¾ **cup (3 ounces) shredded part-skim mozzarella cheese**

¼ **cup shredded Parmesan cheese**

8 **slices pitted black olives**

8 **slices pepperoni (optional)**

1 Preheat air fryer to 400°F; spray basket with nonstick cooking spray.

2 Trim off and discard ends of zucchini. Cut zucchini into 16 (¼-inch-thick) diagonal slices.

3 Combine pizza sauce, tomato paste and oregano in small bowl; mix well. Spread scant teaspoon sauce over each zucchini slice. Combine cheeses in small bowl. Top each zucchini slice with 1 tablespoon cheese mixture, pressing down into sauce. Place 1 olive slice on each of 8 pizza bites. Place 1 folded pepperoni slice on each remaining pizza bite, if desired.

4 Cook in batches 1 to 2 minutes or until cheese is melted. Serve immediately.

MAKES 8 SERVINGS

CALORIES 60 · TOTAL FAT 3.5g · SATURATED FAT 1.5g · CHOLESTEROL 10mg
SODIUM 160mg · CARBOHYDRATE 3g · DIETARY FIBER 1g · PROTEIN 4g

MOZZARELLA STICKS

- ¼ **cup all-purpose flour**
- 2 **eggs**
- 1 **tablespoon water**
- 1 **cup plain dry bread crumbs**
- 2 **teaspoons Italian seasoning**
- ½ **teaspoon salt**
- ½ **teaspoon garlic powder**
- 1 **package (12 ounces) string cheese (12 sticks)**
- 1 **cup marinara or pizza sauce, heated**

1 Place flour in shallow dish. Whisk eggs and water in another shallow dish. Combine bread crumbs, Italian seasoning, salt and garlic powder in third shallow dish.

2 Coat each piece of cheese with flour. Dip in egg mixture, letting excess drip back into dish. Roll in bread crumb mixture to coat. Dip again in egg mixture and roll again in bread crumb mixture. Place on baking sheet. Refrigerate until ready to cook.

3 Preheat air fryer to 370°F. Line basket with parchment paper; spray with nonstick cooking spray.

4 Cook in batches 8 to 10 minutes, shaking halfway through cooking, until golden brown. Serve with marinara sauce.

MAKES 12 SERVINGS

CALORIES 150 · TOTAL FAT 8g · SATURATED FAT 4g · CHOLESTEROL 50mg
SODIUM 440mg · CARBOHYDRATE 10g · DIETARY FIBER 1g · PROTEIN 10g

GARLIC BITES

- **½ of 16-ounce package frozen phyllo dough, thawed to room temperature**
- **¾ cup (1½ sticks) butter, melted**
- **3 large heads garlic, separated into cloves, peeled**
- **½ cup finely chopped walnuts**
- **1 cup Italian-style bread crumbs**

1 Remove phyllo from package; unroll and place on large sheet of waxed paper. Cut phyllo crosswise into 2-inch-wide strips. Cover phyllo with large sheet of plastic wrap and damp, clean kitchen towel. (Phyllo dries out quickly if not covered.)

2 Lay 1 strip of phyllo at a time on flat surface; brush immediately with butter. Place 1 clove of garlic at end. Sprinkle 1 teaspoon walnuts along length of strip.

3 Roll up garlic clove and walnuts in strip, tucking in side edges as you roll. Brush with butter; roll in bread crumbs. Repeat with remaining phyllo, garlic, walnuts, butter and bread crumbs.

4 Preheat air fryer to 350°F. Line basket with parchment paper. Cook in batches 6 to 8 minutes or until golden brown. Cool slightly.

MAKES 24 APPETIZERS

CALORIES 90 · TOTAL FAT 8g · SATURATED FAT 3.5g · CHOLESTEROL 15mg
SODIUM 75mg · CARBOHYDRATE 5g · DIETARY FIBER 0g · PROTEIN 1g

TOASTED RAVIOLI

1 cup all-purpose flour

2 eggs

¼ cup water

1 cup plain dry bread crumbs

1 teaspoon Italian seasoning

¾ teaspoon garlic powder

¼ teaspoon salt

½ cup grated Parmesan cheese

2 tablespoons finely chopped fresh parsley (optional)

1 package (10 ounces) cheese or meat ravioli, thawed if frozen

½ cup pasta sauce, heated

1 Place flour in shallow dish. Whisk eggs and water in another shallow dish. Combine bread crumbs, Italian seasoning, garlic powder and salt in third shallow dish. Combine Parmesan cheese and parsley, if desired, in large bowl.

2 Coat ravioli with flour. Dip in egg mixture, letting excess drip back into dish. Roll in bread crumb mixture to coat. Spray with nonstick cooking spray.

3 Preheat air fryer to 390°F. Poke holes in ravioli with toothpick.

4 Cook in batches 5 to 6 minutes, turning once, until golden brown. Add to bowl with cheese; toss to coat. Serve warm with sauce.

MAKES 6 SERVINGS

CALORIES 300 · TOTAL FAT 6g · SATURATED FAT 4.5g · CHOLESTEROL 115mg
SODIUM 780mg · CARBOHYDRATE 40g · DIETARY FIBER 1g · PROTEIN 15g

MINI CHICKPEA CAKES

1 can (about 15 ounces) chickpeas, rinsed and drained

1 cup grated carrots

⅓ cup seasoned dry bread crumbs

¼ cup creamy Italian salad dressing, plus additional for dipping

1 egg

1 Coarsely mash chickpeas in medium bowl with fork or potato masher. Stir in carrots, bread crumbs, ¼ cup salad dressing and egg; mix well.

2 Shape chickpea mixture into 24 patties, using about 1 tablespoon mixture for each.

3 Preheat air fryer to 370°F. Spray basket with nonstick cooking spray.

4 Cook in batches 10 minutes, turning halfway through cooking, until lightly browned. Serve warm with additional salad dressing for dipping, if desired.

MAKES 2 DOZEN CAKES (ABOUT 8 SERVINGS)

CALORIES 120 · TOTAL FAT 86g · SATURATED FAT 1g · CHOLESTEROL 25mg
SODIUM 240mg · CARBOHYDRATE 12g · DIETARY FIBER 2g · PROTEIN 4g

LAVASH CHIPS WITH ARTICHOKE PESTO

3 pieces lavash bread

¼ cup plus 2 tablespoons olive oil, divided

¾ teaspoon kosher salt, divided

1 can (14 ounces) artichoke hearts, rinsed and drained

½ cup chopped walnuts, toasted*

¼ cup packed fresh basil leaves

1 clove garlic, minced

2 tablespoons lemon juice

¼ cup grated Parmesan cheese

*To toast nuts, cook in preheated 325°F parchment-lined air fryer 3 to 4 minutes or until golden brown.

1 Preheat air fryer to 370°F. Line basket with parchment paper.

2 Brush both sides of lavash with 2 tablespoons oil. Sprinkle with ¼ teaspoon salt. Cut to fit in air fryer, if necessary. Cook in batches 6 to 8 minutes, shaking occasionally, until lavash is crisp and browned. Cool on wire rack.

3 Place artichoke hearts, walnuts, basil, garlic, lemon juice and remaining ½ teaspoon salt in food processor; pulse about 12 times until coarsely chopped. While food processor is running, slowly stream remaining ¼ cup oil until smooth. Add Parmesan cheese and pulse until blended.

4 Serve lavash with pesto.

MAKES 8 SERVINGS (ABOUT 1½ CUPS PESTO)

NOTE: You can also toast walnuts in preheated 350°F oven 6 to 8 minutes, if preferred.

CALORIES 250 · TOTAL FAT 17g · SATURATED FAT 2.5g · CHOLESTEROL 5mg
SODIUM 620mg · CARBOHYDRATE 19g · DIETARY FIBER 1g · PROTEIN 8g

BALSAMIC ONION & PROSCIUTTO PIZZETTES

1 package (about 14 ounces) refrigerated pizza dough

2 tablespoons extra virgin olive oil, divided

1 large or 2 small red onions, cut in half and thinly sliced

¼ teaspoon salt

1½ tablespoons balsamic vinegar

⅛ teaspoon black pepper

⅔ cup grated Parmesan cheese

4 ounces fresh mozzarella cheese, cut into small pieces

1 package (about 3 ounces) thinly sliced prosciutto, cut or torn into small pieces

1 Remove dough from refrigerator; let rest at room temperature while preparing onions. Heat 1 tablespoon oil in medium skillet over medium-high heat. Add onion and salt; cook about 20 minutes or until tender and golden brown, stirring occasionally. Add vinegar and pepper; cook and stir 2 minutes. Set aside to cool.

2 Preheat air fryer to 370°F. Line basket with parchment paper.

3 Divide dough into 16 balls; press into 3-inch rounds (about ⅜ inch thick). Place on baking sheet. Brush rounds with remaining 1 tablespoon oil; sprinkle each with about 1 teaspoon Parmesan cheese. Top with cooked onion, mozzarella cheese, prosciutto and remaining Parmesan cheese.

4 Cook in batches 5 to 7 minutes or until crusts are golden brown.

MAKES 16 PIZZETTES

CALORIES 130 · TOTAL FAT 6g · SATURATED FAT 2.5g · CHOLESTEROL 15mg
SODIUM 360mg · CARBOHYDRATE 13g · DIETARY FIBER 0g · PROTEIN 7g

CRISPY RANCH CHICKEN BITES

1 pound boneless skinless chicken breasts

½ cup ranch dressing, plus additional for serving

1 cup panko bread crumbs

1 Cut chicken into 1-inch cubes. Place ½ cup ranch dressing in small bowl. Spread panko in shallow dish. Dip chicken in dressing; shake off excess. Roll in panko to coat. Spray chicken with nonstick cooking spray.

2 Preheat air fryer to 370°F. Line basket with parchment paper.

3 Cook in batches 8 to 10 minutes or until golden brown and cooked through. Serve with additional ranch dressing.

MAKES 6 SERVINGS

CALORIES 210 · TOTAL FAT 9g · SATURATED FAT 1.5g · CHOLESTEROL 60mg
SODIUM 230mg · CARBOHYDRATE 11g · DIETARY FIBER 0g · PROTEIN 18g

MINI EGG ROLLS

½ **pound ground pork**

3 **cloves garlic, minced**

1 **teaspoon minced fresh ginger**

¼ **teaspoon red pepper flakes**

6 **cups (12 ounces) shredded coleslaw mix**

¼ **cup reduced-sodium soy sauce**

1 **tablespoon cornstarch**

1 **tablespoon seasoned rice vinegar**

½ **cup chopped green onions**

28 **wonton wrappers**

Prepared sweet and sour sauce

Chinese hot mustard

1   Combine pork, garlic, ginger and red pepper flakes in large nonstick skillet; cook and stir over medium heat about 4 minutes or until pork is cooked through, stirring to break up meat. Add coleslaw mix; cover and cook 2 minutes. Uncover and cook 2 minutes or until coleslaw mix just begins to wilt.

2   Whisk soy sauce and cornstarch in small bowl until smooth and well blended; stir into pork mixture. Add vinegar; cook 2 to 3 minutes or until sauce is thickened. Remove from heat; stir in green onions.

3   Working with 1 wonton wrapper at a time, place wrapper on clean work surface. Spoon 1 level tablespoon pork mixture across and just below center of wrapper. Fold bottom point of wrapper up over filling; fold side points over filling, forming envelope shape. Moisten inside edges of top point with water and roll egg roll toward top point, pressing firmly to seal. Repeat with remaining wrappers and filling. Spray egg rolls with nonstick cooking spray.

4   Preheat air fryer to 370°F. Cook in batches 3 to 5 minutes or until golden brown. Remove to cooling rack; cool slightly before serving. Serve with sweet and sour sauce and mustard for dipping.

MAKES 28 MINI EGG ROLLS

CALORIES 50 · TOTAL FAT 2g · SATURATED FAT 0.5g · CHOLESTEROL 5mg
SODIUM 140mg · CARBOHYDRATE 6g · DIETARY FIBER 0g · PROTEIN 2g

CHILI PUFFS

1 **sheet frozen puff pastry (half of 17¼-ounce package), thawed**

1 **can (about 15 ounces) chili without beans**

4 **ounces cream cheese, softened**

¼ **cup (1 ounce) finely shredded sharp Cheddar cheese**

Sliced green onions (optional)

1 Spray 2½-inch silicone muffin cups with nonstick cooking spray.

2 Roll out puff pastry on lightly floured surface. Cut nine (3-inch) squares. Press dough into muffin cups.

3 Preheat air fryer to 390°F. Cook in batches 6 to 8 minutes or until golden brown. Cool slightly.

4 Meanwhile, combine chili and cream cheese in small saucepan over medium-low heat. Heat, stirring occasionally, until warmed and cream cheese blends into chili mixture. Remove from heat.

5 Fill each pastry shell with 2 teaspoons chili mixture, pressing down centers of pastry to fill, if necessary. Sprinkle evenly with Cheddar cheese. Garnish with green onions, if desired.

MAKES 9 PUFFS

TIP: Use a pizza cutter to easily cut puff pastry sheets.

CALORIES 110 · TOTAL FAT 8g · SATURATED FAT 4g · CHOLESTEROL 20mg
SODIUM 290mg · CARBOHYDRATE 7g · DIETARY FIBER 0g · PROTEIN 5g

TURKEY MEATBALLS WITH YOGURT-CUCUMBER SAUCE

1 **pound lean ground turkey or chicken**

1 **cup finely chopped onion**

½ **cup plain dry bread crumbs**

¼ **cup whipping cream**

2 **cloves garlic, minced**

1 **egg, lightly beaten**

3 **tablespoons chopped fresh mint**

1 **teaspoon salt**

¼ **teaspoon ground red pepper**

1 **tablespoon olive oil**

Yogurt-Cucumber Sauce (recipe follows)

1 Combine turkey, onion, bread crumbs, cream, garlic, egg, mint, salt and ground red pepper in large bowl; mix well. Shape into 30 meatballs. Place meatballs on baking sheet. Cover with plastic wrap; refrigerate 1 hour.

2 Preheat air fryer to 390°F. Line basket with parchment paper; spray with nonstick cooking spray.

3 Brush meatballs with oil. Cook in batches 12 to 14 minutes, shaking halfway through cooking, until cooked through.

4 Meanwhile, prepare Yogurt-Cucumber Sauce. Serve meatballs with sauce.

**MAKES 30 MEATBALLS
(2 MEATBALLS PER SERVING)**

YOGURT-CUCUMBER SAUCE

1 **container (6 ounces) plain nonfat Greek yogurt**

½ **cup peeled seeded and finely chopped cucumber**

2 **teaspoons chopped fresh mint**

2 **teaspoons grated lemon peel**

2 **teaspoons lemon juice**

¼ **teaspoon salt**

Combine all ingredients in small bowl. Refrigerate until ready to serve.

MAKES ABOUT 1 CUP

CALORIES 90 · TOTAL FAT 3.5g · SATURATED FAT 1g · CHOLESTEROL 30mg
SODIUM 250mg · CARBOHYDRATE 5g · DIETARY FIBER 0g · PROTEIN 10g

CAPRESE-STYLE TARTLETS

3 tomatoes, cut into 4 slices each

3 tablespoons prepared pesto

1 sheet frozen puff pastry (half of 17¼-ounce package)

6 ounces fresh mozzarella cheese

2 tablespoons chopped kalamata olives

1 Place tomatoes in large resealable food storage bag. Add pesto; toss to coat. Marinate at room temperature 30 minutes.

2 Unfold puff pastry; thaw 20 minutes on lightly floured surface.

3 Preheat air fryer to 370°F. Line basket with parchment paper.

4 Cut out six (4-inch) rounds from pastry. Top each round with two tomato slices. Cook in batches 8 to 10 minutes or until pastry is light golden and puffed.

5 Cut cheese into six (¼-inch-thick) slices. Top each tart with 1 cheese slice. Cook in batches 1 minute or until cheese is melted. Top tarts evenly with olives. Serve warm.

MAKES 6 TARTLETS

CALORIES 160 · TOTAL FAT 11g · SATURATED FAT 5g · CHOLESTEROL 20mg
SODIUM 250mg · CARBOHYDRATE 6g · DIETARY FIBER 1g · PROTEIN 7g

BUFFALO CAULIFLOWER BITES

½ cup all-purpose flour

½ cup water

½ teaspoon garlic powder

½ teaspoon salt

¼ teaspoon black pepper

1 small head cauliflower, cut into small florets

3 tablespoons hot pepper sauce

1 tablespoon melted butter

Chopped fresh parsley

Blue cheese dressing and celery sticks (optional)

1 Preheat air fryer to 390°F. Line basket with parchment paper.

2 Combine flour, water, garlic powder, salt and pepper in large bowl; stir until mixed. Add cauliflower; stir until florets are well coated.

3 Cook 12 to 15 minutes, shaking occasionally during cooking, until florets are slightly tender and browned.

4 Meanwhile, combine hot pepper sauce and butter in medium bowl. Add warm florets; toss well.

5 Sprinkle with parsley. Serve with blue cheese dressing and celery sticks, if desired.

MAKES 4 SERVINGS

CALORIES 80 · TOTAL FAT 0.5g · SATURATED FAT 0g · CHOLESTEROL 0mg
SODIUM 690mg · CARBOHYDRATE 16g · DIETARY FIBER 2g · PROTEIN 3g

BAKED ORANGE BRIE APPETIZER

1 **sheet puff pastry (half of 17¼-ounce package), thawed**

⅓ **cup orange marmalade**

2 **tablespoons chopped pecans (optional)**

1 **round (8 ounces) Brie cheese**

1 **egg white, beaten**

1 Roll out puff pastry to 12-inch square. Use knife to cut off four corners; set aside scraps.

2 Spread marmalade over center of pastry to 1 inch of edges. Sprinkle pecans over marmalade, if desired. Place Brie in center on top of pecans. Brush exposed dough with egg white.

3 Gather up edges of puff pastry and bring together over center of Brie, covering cheese entirely. Pinch and twist pastry edges together to seal. Use dough scraps to decorate top of Brie. Brush lightly with egg white.

4 Preheat air fryer to 370°F.

5 Cook 8 to 10 minutes or until golden brown. Serve warm.

MAKES 6 SERVINGS

CALORIES 200 · TOTAL FAT 12g · SATURATED FAT 7g · CHOLESTEROL 40mg
SODIUM 270mg · CARBOHYDRATE 15g · DIETARY FIBER 0g · PROTEIN 9g

GREEN BEAN DIPPERS

1 egg

1 pound green beans, ends trimmed

½ cup plain dry bread crumbs

2 tablespoons grated Parmesan cheese

1 tablespoon olive oil

½ teaspoon garlic powder

¼ teaspoon salt

Prepared salad dressing (optional)

1   Whisk egg in large bowl. Add green beans; toss to coat. Combine bread crumbs, Parmesan cheese, oil, garlic powder and salt in small bowl. Sprinkle bread crumb mixture over green beans.

2   Preheat air fryer to 390°F. Line basket with parchment paper.

3   Cook in batches 8 to 10 minutes, shaking occasionally during cooking, until crispy. Serve with dressing, if desired.

MAKES 6 SERVINGS

CALORIES 100 · TOTAL FAT 4.5g · SATURATED FAT 1g · CHOLESTEROL 35mg
SODIUM 220mg · CARBOHYDRATE 12g · DIETARY FIBER 2g · PROTEIN 5g

PUNCHED PIZZA ROUNDS

1 package (12 ounces) refrigerated flaky buttermilk biscuits (10 biscuits)

1 package (5 ounces) pepperoni slices

¼ cup chopped bell pepper (optional)

1 tablespoon dried basil

½ cup pizza sauce

1½ cups (6 ounces) shredded mozzarella cheese

Shredded Parmesan cheese (optional)

1 Spray (2½-inch) silicone muffin cups with nonstick cooking spray.

2 Separate biscuits; split each biscuit in half horizontally to create 20 rounds. Place in prepared muffin cups. Press 4 mini pepperoni slices into center of each round. Sprinkle with bell pepper, if desired, and basil. Spread pizza sauce over pepperoni; sprinkle with mozzarella.

3 Preheat air fryer to 370°F. Cook in batches 14 to 16 minutes or until pizzas are golden brown. Sprinkle with Parmesan cheese, if desired. Cool 2 minutes; remove to wire racks. Serve warm.

MAKES 20 SERVINGS

CALORIES 110 · TOTAL FAT 6g · SATURATED FAT 3g · CHOLESTEROL 15mg
SODIUM 360mg · CARBOHYDRATE 9g · DIETARY FIBER 0g · PROTEIN 5g

FALAFEL NUGGETS

SAUCE

- **2½ cups tomato sauce**
- **⅓ cup tomato paste**
- **2 tablespoons lemon juice**
- **2 teaspoons sugar**
- **1 teaspoon onion powder**
- **½ teaspoon salt**

FALAFEL

- **2 cans (about 15 ounces each) chickpeas, rinsed and drained**
- **½ cup all-purpose flour**
- **½ cup chopped fresh parsley**
- **1 egg**
- **¼ cup minced onion**
- **3 tablespoons lemon juice**
- **2 tablespoons minced garlic**
- **2 teaspoons ground cumin**
- **½ teaspoon salt**
- **½ teaspoon ground red pepper *or* red pepper flakes**

1 For sauce, combine tomato sauce, tomato paste, 2 tablespoons lemon juice, sugar, onion powder and ½ teaspoon salt in medium saucepan. Simmer over medium-low heat 20 minutes or until heated through. Cover and keep warm until ready to serve.

2 For falafel, combine chickpeas, flour, parsley, egg, minced onion, 3 tablespoons lemon juice, garlic, cumin, ½ teaspoon salt and ground red pepper in food processor or blender; process until well blended. Shape mixture into 1-inch balls. Spray with nonstick cooking spray.

3 Preheat air fryer to 390°F. Line basket with foil; spray with cooking spray.

4 Cook in batches 12 to 15 minutes, turning halfway through cooking, until browned. Serve with sauce.

MAKES 12 SERVINGS

CALORIES 120 · TOTAL FAT 2g · SATURATED FAT 0g · CHOLESTEROL 15mg
SODIUM 660mg · CARBOHYDRATE 20g · DIETARY FIBER 5g · PROTEIN 6g

SANDWICHES & LIGHTER FARE

OPEN-FACED MINI BLUE CHEESE BURGERS

1 large onion, thinly sliced

1 teaspoon olive oil

1 package (20 ounces) lean ground turkey

¼ teaspoon garlic salt

1½ tablespoons Dijon mustard

¼ cup crumbled blue cheese

4 lettuce leaves, torn into 12 pieces

6 whole wheat mini sandwich thin rounds, split and toasted

1. Preheat air fryer to 390°F. Spray basket with nonstick cooking spray.

2. Toss onion with oil in medium bowl. Cook 6 to 8 minutes, shaking halfway through cooking, until onions are golden brown. Remove from basket; set aside.

3. Combine ground turkey and garlic salt in medium bowl. Shape turkey into 12 (¼-inch-thick) patties.

4. Cook burgers in batches 8 to 10 minutes or until cooked through.

5. Combine mustard and blue cheese in small bowl. Place 1 lettuce leaf on bottom of each sandwich thin; top with burger, blue cheese mixture and onions.

MAKES 12 BURGERS

CALORIES 120 • TOTAL FAT 2g • SATURATED FAT 0g • CHOLESTEROL 25mg
SODIUM 210mg • CARBOHYDRATE 12g • DIETARY FIBER 0g • PROTEIN 14g

BUFFALO CHICKEN WRAPS

2 boneless skinless chicken breasts (about 4 ounces each)

4 tablespoons buffalo wing sauce, divided

1 cup broccoli slaw

1½ teaspoons light blue cheese salad dressing

2 (8-inch) whole wheat tortillas, warmed

1 Place chicken in large resealable food storage bag. Add 2 tablespoons buffalo sauce; seal bag. Marinate in refrigerator 15 minutes.

2 Preheat air fryer to 370°F. Cook 8 to 10 minutes per side or until no longer pink in center. When cool enough to handle, slice chicken; combine with remaining 2 tablespoons buffalo sauce in medium bowl.

3 Combine broccoli slaw and blue cheese dressing in medium bowl; mix well.

4 Arrange chicken and broccoli slaw evenly down center of each tortilla. Roll up to secure filling. To serve, cut in half diagonally.

MAKES 2 SERVINGS

TIP: If you do not like the spicy flavor of buffalo wing sauce, substitute your favorite barbecue sauce.

CALORIES 340 · TOTAL FAT 7g · SATURATED FAT 1.5g · CHOLESTEROL 85mg
SODIUM 730mg · CARBOHYDRATE 38g · DIETARY FIBER 0g · PROTEIN 31g

LENTIL BURGERS

1 can (about 14 ounces) vegetable broth

1 cup dried lentils, rinsed and sorted

1 small carrot, grated

¼ cup coarsely chopped mushrooms

1 egg

¼ cup plain dry bread crumbs

3 tablespoons finely chopped onion

2 to 4 cloves garlic, minced

1 teaspoon dried thyme

¼ cup plain nonfat yogurt

¼ cup chopped seeded cucumber

½ teaspoon dried mint

¼ teaspoon dried dill weed

¼ teaspoon black pepper

⅛ teaspoon salt

Dash hot pepper sauce (optional)

Kaiser rolls (optional)

1 Bring broth to a boil in medium saucepan over high heat. Stir in lentils; reduce heat to low. Simmer, covered, about 30 minutes or until lentils are tender and liquid is absorbed. Cool to room temperature.

2 Place lentils, carrot and mushrooms in food processor or blender; process until finely chopped but not smooth. (Some whole lentils should still be visible.) Stir in egg, bread crumbs, onion, garlic and thyme. Cover and refrigerate 2 to 3 hours.

3 Shape lentil mixture into four (½-inch-thick) patties.

4 Preheat air fryer to 390°F. Spray basket with nonstick cooking spray. Cook patties in batches 8 to 10 minutes or until browned.

5 Meanwhile, for sauce, combine yogurt, cucumber, mint, dill weed, black pepper, salt and hot pepper sauce, if desired, in small bowl. Serve burgers on rolls with sauce.

MAKES 4 SERVINGS

CALORIES 240 · TOTAL FAT 2g · SATURATED FAT 0.5g · CHOLESTEROL 45mg
SODIUM 210mg · CARBOHYDRATE 41g · DIETARY FIBER 7g · PROTEIN 15g

SALMON CROQUETTES

1 **can (14¾ ounces) pink salmon, drained and flaked**

½ **cup mashed potatoes***

1 **egg, beaten**

3 **tablespoons diced red bell pepper**

2 **tablespoons sliced green onion**

1 **tablespoon chopped fresh parsley**

½ **cup seasoned dry bread crumbs**

*Use mashed potatoes that are freshly made, leftover, or potatoes made from instant potatoes.

1 Combine salmon, potatoes, egg, bell pepper, green onion and parsley in medium bowl; mix well.

2 Place bread crumbs on medium plate. Shape salmon mixture into 10 croquettes about 3 inches long by 1 inch wide. Roll croquettes in bread crumbs to coat. Place on baking sheet. Refrigerate 15 to 20 minutes or until firm.

3 Preheat air fryer to 350°F. Cook in batches 6 to 8 minutes or until browned. Serve immediately.

MAKES 5 SERVINGS (2 PER SERVING)

CALORIES 200 · TOTAL FAT 6g · SATURATED FAT 1.5g · CHOLESTEROL 110mg
SODIUM 560mg · CARBOHYDRATE 12g · DIETARY FIBER 0g · PROTEIN 24g

TASTY TURKEY TURNOVERS

1 **package (about 8 ounces) refrigerated crescent roll sheet**

2 **tablespoons honey mustard, plus addtional for serving**

3 **ounces thinly sliced lean deli turkey breast**

¾ **cup packaged broccoli coleslaw mix**

1 **egg white, beaten**

1 Roll out dough onto lightly floured surface. Using a wide glass or cookie cutter, cut into 3½-inch circles. Spread 2 tablespoons honey mustard lightly over dough circles; top with turkey and coleslaw mix. Brush edges of dough with beaten egg white. Fold circles in half; press edges with tines of fork to seal. Brush with egg white.

2 Preheat air fryer to 370°F. Spray basket with nonstick cooking spray.

3 Cook in batches 6 to 7 minutes or until golden brown. Let stand 5 minutes before serving. Serve warm or at room temperature with additional honey mustard for dipping, if desired.

MAKES 6 SERVINGS

CALORIES 160 · TOTAL FAT 7g · SATURATED FAT 0g · CHOLESTEROL 5mg
SODIUM 440mg · CARBOHYDRATE 19g · DIETARY FIBER 0g · PROTEIN 6g

CAPRESE PORTOBELLO BURGERS

4 **portobello mushrooms (about ¾ pound), gills and stems removed**

3 **ounces mozzarella cheese, diced**

2 **plum tomatoes, chopped**

2 **tablespoons chopped fresh basil**

1 **tablespoon light balsamic vinaigrette**

1 **clove garlic, crushed**

⅛ **teaspoon black pepper**

4 **whole wheat sandwich thin rounds, toasted**

1. Preheat air fryer to 350°F. Spray basket with nonstick cooking spray. Cook mushrooms in batches 5 to 7 minutes or until slightly tender.

2. Combine cheese, tomatoes, basil, vinaigrette, garlic and pepper in small bowl. Spoon one fourth of tomato mixture into each cap. Cook 2 to 3 minutes or until is cheese melted. Serve on sandwich thins.

MAKES 4 SERVINGS

NOTE: Cooked portobello mushrooms can be frozen and will keep for several months. Store in plastic containers or freezer bags.

CALORIES 180 · TOTAL FAT 5g · SATURATED FAT 2g · CHOLESTEROL 15mg
SODIUM 340mg · CARBOHYDRATE 28g · DIETARY FIBER 1g · PROTEIN 12g

VEGETABLE AND HUMMUS MUFFALETTA

1 small eggplant, cut lengthwise into ⅛-inch slices

1 yellow squash, cut lengthwise into ⅛-inch slices

1 zucchini, cut on the diagonal into ⅛-inch slices

1 tablespoon extra virgin olive oil

¼ teaspoon salt

¼ teaspoon black pepper

1 boule or round bread (8 inches), cut in half horizontally

1 container (8 ounces) hummus, any flavor

1 jar (12 ounces) roasted red bell peppers, drained

1 jar (6 ounces) marinated artichoke hearts, drained and chopped

1 small tomato, thinly sliced

1. Combine eggplant, squash, zucchini, oil, salt and black pepper in large bowl; toss to coat.

2. Preheat air fryer to 390°F. Cook vegetables in batches 4 to 6 minutes, shaking halfway during cooking, until tender and golden. Cool to room temperature.

3. Scoop out bread from both halves of boule, leaving about 1 inch of bread on edges and about 1½ inches on bottom. (Reserve bread for bread crumbs or croutons.) Spread hummus evenly on inside bottom of bread. Layer vegetables, roasted peppers, artichokes and tomato over hummus; cover with top half of bread. Wrap stuffed loaf tightly in plastic wrap. Refrigerate at least 1 hour before cutting into wedges.

MAKES 8 SERVINGS

SUBSTITUTION: You can substitute a red bell pepper for the jarred peppers and roast it in the air fryer. Preheat air fryer to 390°F. Cook 15 minutes, turning once or twice. Let sit in air fryer 10 minutes longer to loosen skin. Carefully remove skin with paring knife.

CALORIES 270 · TOTAL FAT 7g · SATURATED FAT 1g · CHOLESTEROL 0mg
SODIUM 720mg · CARBOHYDRATE 44g · DIETARY FIBER 3g · PROTEIN 8g

TUNA MELTS

1 can (about 5 ounces) chunk white tuna packed in water, drained and flaked

½ cup packaged coleslaw mix

1 tablespoon sliced green onion

1 tablespoon light mayonnaise

½ tablespoon Dijon mustard

¼ teaspoon dried dill weed (optional)

2 English muffins, split

¼ cup (1 ounce) shredded reduced-fat Cheddar cheese

1 Combine tuna, coleslaw mix and green onion in medium bowl. Combine mayonnaise, mustard and dill weed, if desired, in small bowl. Stir mayonnaise mixture into tuna mixture. Spread tuna mixture onto muffin halves.

2 Preheat air fryer to 370°F. Cook 3 to 4 minutes or until heated through and lightly browned. Sprinkle with cheese. Cook 1 to 2 minutes until cheese melts.

MAKES 2 SERVINGS

CALORIES 260 · TOTAL FAT 7g · SATURATED FAT 5g · CHOLESTEROL 40mg
SODIUM 690mg · CARBOHYDRATE 27g · DIETARY FIBER 0g · PROTEIN 22g

FOCACCIA BARS

2 **tablespoons olive oil**

1 **large red or yellow bell pepper, thinly sliced**

 Cornmeal

1 **package (11 ounces) refrigerated French bread dough**

¼ **teaspoon coarse salt**

⅛ **teaspoon dried oregano**

¼ **cup (1 ounce) shredded Italian cheese blend**

1 Heat oil in medium skillet over medium-high heat. Add bell pepper; cook and stir 3 to 5 minutes or until pepper is tender and lightly browned. Remove from skillet, reserving oil.

2 Sprinkle cornmeal on work surface. Shape dough into 16×4-inch rectangle, then into four (4-inch) squares.

3 Press fingertips into dough to create dimples. Drizzle leftover oil from skillet onto dough. Spread pepper slices over dough. Sprinkle with salt and oregano. Top with cheese.

4 Preheat air fryer to 370°F. Cook in batches 8 to 10 minutes or until cheese melts and bread is golden brown. Let focaccia rest 2 to 3 minutes. Serve warm or at room temperature.

MAKES 4 SERVINGS

NOTE: Refrigerate leftovers up to 2 days or freeze up to 1 month.

CALORIES 270 · TOTAL FAT 11g · SATURATED FAT 2g · CHOLESTEROL 5mg
SODIUM 510mg · CARBOHYDRATE 38g · DIETARY FIBER 1g · PROTEIN 8g

SPICY EGGPLANT BURGERS

1 **eggplant (about 1¼ pounds)**

2 **egg whites**

½ **cup Italian-style panko bread crumbs**

3 **tablespoons chipotle mayonnaise or regular mayonnaise**

4 **whole wheat hamburger buns, warmed**

1½ **cups loosely packed baby spinach**

8 **thin slices tomato**

4 **slices pepper jack cheese**

1 Cut four (½-inch-thick) slices from widest part of eggplant. Beat egg whites in shallow dish. Place panko on medium plate.

2 Dip eggplant slices in egg whites; dredge in panko, pressing gently to adhere. Spray with nonstick cooking spray.

3 Preheat air fryer to 370°F. Line basket with foil. Cook in batches 8 to 10 minutes, flipping halfway through cooking, or until golden brown.

4 Spread mayonnaise on bottom halves of buns; top with spinach, tomatoes, eggplant, cheese and tops of buns.

MAKES 4 SERVINGS

CALORIES 350 · TOTAL FAT 14g · SATURATED FAT 4g · CHOLESTEROL 15mg
SODIUM 450mg · CARBOHYDRATE 41g · DIETARY FIBER 5g · PROTEIN 10g

BAKED PORK BUNS

1 tablespoon oil

2 cups coarsely chopped bok choy

1 small onion or large shallot, thinly sliced

1 container (18 ounces) refrigerated shredded barbecue pork

2 packages (10 ounces each) refrigerated jumbo buttermilk biscuit dough (5 biscuits per package)

1 Heat oil in large skillet over medium-high heat. Add bok choy and onion; cook and stir 8 to 10 minutes or until vegetables are tender. Remove from heat; stir in barbecue pork.

2 Lightly flour work surface. Separate biscuits; split each biscuit in half to create two thin biscuits. Flatten each biscuit half into 5-inch circle.

3 Spoon heaping tablespoon of pork mixture onto one side of each circle. Fold dough over filling to form half circle; press edges to seal.

4 Preheat air fryer to 350°F. Line basket with parchment paper; spray with nonstick cooking spray.

5 Cook in batches 8 to 10 minutes or until golden brown.

MAKES 10 SERVINGS

CALORIES 240 · TOTAL FAT 8g · SATURATED FAT 3g · CHOLESTEROL 20mg
SODIUM 860mg · CARBOHYDRATE 34g · DIETARY FIBER 0g · PROTEIN 10g

TUNA MONTE CRISTO SANDWICHES

¼ **pound deli tuna salad**

4 **oval slices sourdough or challah (egg) bread**

2 **slices (1 ounce each) Cheddar cheese**

¼ **cup reduced-fat (2%) milk**

1 **egg**

1   Spread tuna salad evenly over 2 bread slices; top with cheese and remaining bread slices.

2   Combine milk and egg in shallow bowl; stir until well blended. Brush sandwiches with egg mixture. Spray with nonstick cooking spray.

3   Preheat air fryer to 370°F. Cook 4 to 5 minutes, flipping over halfway during cooking, until cheese melts and sandwiches are golden brown.

MAKES 2 SERVINGS

SERVING SUGGESTION: Serve with a chilled fruit salad.

CALORIES 410 · TOTAL FAT 17g · SATURATED FAT 7g · CHOLESTEROL 140mg
SODIUM 910mg · CARBOHYDRATE 40g · DIETARY FIBER 0g · PROTEIN 27g

SPINACH & ROASTED PEPPER PANINI

1 loaf (12 ounces) focaccia

1½ cups spinach leaves (about 12 leaves)

1 jar (about 7 ounces) roasted red peppers, drained

4 ounces fontina cheese, thinly sliced

¾ cup thinly sliced red onion

Olive oil (optional)

1. Cut focaccia in half horizontally. Layer bottom half with spinach, roasted peppers, cheese and onion. Cover with top half of focaccia. Brush outsides of sandwich lightly with oil, if desired. Cut sandwich into six equal pieces.

2. Preheat air fryer to 370°F. Line basket with parchment paper. Cook in batches 3 to 5 minutes or until cheese melts and bread is golden brown.

MAKES 6 SERVINGS

NOTE: Focaccia can be found in the bakery section of most supermarkets. It is often available in different flavors, such as tomato, herb, cheese or onion.

CALORIES 220 · TOTAL FAT 10g · SATURATED FAT 3g · CHOLESTEROL 15mg
SODIUM 570mg · CARBOHYDRATE 23g · DIETARY FIBER 1g · PROTEIN 10g

VEGGIE PIZZA PITAS

1 **whole wheat pita bread round, cut in half horizontally (to make 2 rounds)**

2 **tablespoons pizza sauce**

½ **teaspoon dried basil**

⅛ **teaspoon red pepper flakes (optional)**

½ **cup sliced mushrooms**

¼ **cup thinly sliced green bell pepper**

¼ **cup thinly sliced red onion**

½ **cup (4 ounces) shredded mozzarella cheese**

1 **teaspoon grated Parmesan cheese**

1 Arrange pita rounds, rough sides up, in single layer on parchment paper. Spread 1 tablespoon pizza sauce evenly over each round to within ¼ inch of edge. Sprinkle with basil and red pepper flakes, if desired. Top with mushrooms, bell pepper and onion. Sprinkle with mozzarella cheese.

2 Preheat air fryer to 370°F.

3 Cook 5 to 7 minutes until mozzarella cheese melts. Sprinkle ½ teaspoon Parmesan cheese over each pita round.

MAKES 2 SERVINGS

CALORIES 150 · TOTAL FAT 6g · SATURATED FAT 3.5g · CHOLESTEROL 20mg
SODIUM 370mg · CARBOHYDRATE 14g · DIETARY FIBER 1g · PROTEIN 10g

MOZZARELLA & ROASTED RED PEPPER SANDWICH

1 tablespoon olive oil vinaigrette or Italian salad dressing

2 slices Italian-style sandwich bread (2 ounces)

2 fresh basil leaves

⅓ cup roasted red peppers, rinsed, drained and patted dry

1 to 2 slices (1 ounce each) part-skim mozzarella or Swiss cheese

1 Brush dressing on 1 side of 1 bread slice; top with basil, roasted peppers, cheese and remaining bread slice. Lightly spray both sides of sandwich with nonstick cooking spray.

2 Preheat air fryer to 350°F. Cook 4 to 5 minutes, turning halfway through cooking, until cheese melts and bread is golden brown.

MAKES 1 SERVING

CALORIES 303 · TOTAL FAT 9g · SATURATED FAT 5g · CHOLESTEROL 25mg
SODIUM 727mg · CARBOHYDRATE 35g · DIETARY FIBER 2g · PROTEIN 16g

DINNER WINNERS

STEAK, MUSHROOMS & ONIONS

¾ **pound boneless steak, cut into 1-inch cubes**

8 **ounces sliced mushrooms, cleaned and washed**

1 **small onion, chopped**

3 **tablespoons melted butter, divided**

1 **teaspoon Worcestershire sauce**

½ **teaspoon garlic powder**

½ **teaspoon salt**

¼ **teaspoon black pepper**

 Hot cooked egg noodles

½ **teaspoon dried parsley flakes**

1 Combine steak pieces, mushrooms and onion in large bowl. Toss with 1½ tablespoons butter, Worcestershire sauce and garlic powder.

2 Preheat air fryer to 390°F. Cook steak mixture 10 to 12 minutes, shaking occasionally, until steak is cooked through.

3 Remove steak mixture to large bowl. Toss with remaining 1½ tablespoons butter, salt and pepper.

4 Serve over noodles. Sprinkle with parsley flakes.

MAKES 4 SERVINGS

CALORIES 300 • TOTAL FAT 25g • SATURATED FAT 1g • CHOLESTEROL 70mg
SODIUM 360mg • CARBOHYDRATE 4g • DIETARY FIBER 1g • PROTEIN 17g

DILLED SALMON IN PARCHMENT

2 **skinless salmon fillets (4 ounces each)**

1 **tablespoon butter, melted**

1 **tablespoon lemon juice**

1 **tablespoon chopped fresh dill**

1 **tablespoon chopped shallots**

¼ **teaspoon salt**

⅛ **teaspoon black pepper**

1 Preheat air fryer to 370°F. Cut two pieces of parchment paper into 12-inch squares. Place fish fillets on parchment.

2 Combine butter and lemon juice in small bowl; drizzle over fish. Sprinkle with dill, shallots, salt and pepper. Wrap parchment around fish.

3 Cook 8 to 10 minutes or until fish is cooked through and easily flakes when tested with a fork.

MAKES 2 SERVINGS

CALORIES 290 · TOTAL FAT 21g · SATURATED FAT 7g · CHOLESTEROL 80mg
SODIUM 360mg · CARBOHYDRATE 1g · DIETARY FIBER 0g · PROTEIN 23g

JAPANESE FRIED CHICKEN ON WATERCRESS

1 pound boneless skinless chicken breasts, cut into 2-inch pieces

2 tablespoons tamari or soy sauce

1 tablespoon sake

3 cloves garlic, minced

1 teaspoon minced fresh ginger

¼ cup cornstarch

2 tablespoons all-purpose flour

SALAD

¼ cup unseasoned rice vinegar

3 teaspoons tamari or soy sauce

1 teaspoon dark sesame oil

2 bunches watercress, trimmed of tough stems

1 pint grape tomatoes, halved

1 Place chicken in large resealable food storage bag. Mix 2 tablespoons tamari, sake, garlic and ginger in small bowl. Pour over chicken and marinate in refrigerator at least 30 minutes, turning bag occasionally.

2 Combine cornstarch and flour in shallow dish. Drain chicken and discard marinade. Roll chicken pieces in cornstarch mixture and shake off excess.

3 Preheat air fryer to 370°F. Cook in batches 8 to 10 minutes or until chicken is golden brown.

4 For salad, whisk together vinegar, 3 teaspoons tamari and sesame oil in small bowl. Arrange watercress and tomatoes on serving plates. Drizzle with dressing and top with chicken.

MAKES 4 SERVINGS

CALORIES 260 · TOTAL FAT 4g · SATURATED FAT 1g · CHOLESTEROL 85mg
SODIUM 620mg · CARBOHYDRATE 28g · DIETARY FIBER 2g · PROTEIN 29g

GREEK CHICKEN BURGERS WITH CUCUMBER YOGURT SAUCE

½ cup plus 2 tablespoons plain nonfat Greek yogurt

½ medium cucumber, peeled, seeded and finely chopped

Juice of ½ lemon

3 cloves garlic, minced and divided

2 teaspoons finely chopped fresh mint *or* ½ teaspoon dried mint

⅛ teaspoon salt

⅛ teaspoon ground white pepper

BURGERS

1 pound ground chicken breast

3 ounces reduced-fat crumbled feta cheese

4 large kalamata olives, rinsed, patted dry and minced

1 egg

½ to 1 teaspoon dried oregano

¼ teaspoon black pepper

Mixed baby lettuce (optional)

Fresh mint leaves (optional)

1 Combine yogurt, cucumber, lemon juice, 2 cloves garlic, 2 teaspoons chopped mint, salt and white pepper in medium bowl; mix well. Cover and refrigerate until ready to serve.

2 For burgers, combine chicken, feta cheese, olives, egg, oregano, black pepper and remaining 1 clove garlic in large bowl; mix well. Shape mixture into four patties.

3 Preheat air fryer to 370°F. Spray basket with nonstick cooking spray. Cook 12 to 15 minutes or until cooked through (165°F).

4 Serve burgers with sauce and mixed greens, if desired. Garnish with mint leaves.

MAKES 4 SERVINGS

CALORIES 270 · TOTAL FAT 12g · SATURATED FAT 4g · CHOLESTEROL 110mg
SODIUM 430mg · CARBOHYDRATE 6g · DIETARY FIBER 0g · PROTEIN 31g

SPICY LEMONY ALMOND CHICKEN

½ teaspoon paprika

½ teaspoon black pepper

¼ teaspoon salt

4 boneless skinless chicken breasts (about 1 pound), flattened to ¼-inch thickness

1 ounce slivered almonds, toasted*

¼ cup water

2 tablespoons lemon juice

2 tablespoons butter or margarine

2 teaspoons Worcestershire sauce

½ teaspoon grated lemon peel

To toast almonds in air fryer, cook in small dish or ramekin about 5 minutes or until lightly browned and fragrant, shaking frequently. To toast almonds in skillet, cook about 5 minutes or until lightly browned and fragrant, stirring frequently.

1 Combine paprika, pepper and salt in small bowl; sprinkle evenly over both sides of chicken.

2 Preheat air fryer to 370°F. Spray basket with nonstick cooking spray. Cook chicken 12 to 15 minutes or until lightly browned and no longer pink in center. Set aside on serving platter; sprinkle with almonds. Cover to keep warm.

3 Combine water, lemon juice, butter and Worcestershire sauce in small skillet over medium-high heat. Cook and stir until sauce is reduced to ¼ cup. Remove from heat, stir in lemon peel; spoon evenly over chicken.

MAKES 4 SERVINGS

TIP: To pound chicken, place between two pieces of plastic wrap. Starting in the center, pound chicken with a meat mallet to reach an even thickness.

CALORIES 193 · TOTAL FAT 7g · SATURATED FAT 1g · CHOLESTEROL 66mg
SODIUM 257mg · CARBOHYDRATE 3g · DIETARY FIBER 1g · PROTEIN 28g

FRIED TOFU WITH ASIAN VEGETABLES

1 **pound firm tofu**

¼ **cup soy sauce, divided**

1 **cup all-purpose flour**

⅛ **teaspoon black pepper**

1 **package (16 ounces) frozen mixed Asian vegetables***

3 **tablespoons water**

1 **teaspoon cornstarch**

3 **tablespoons plum sauce**

2 **tablespoons lemon juice**

2 **teaspoons sugar**

1 **teaspoon minced fresh ginger**

⅛ **to ¼ teaspoon red pepper flakes**

Frozen vegetables do not need to be thawed before cooking.

1 Drain tofu; cut into ¾-inch cubes. Gently mix tofu and 2 tablespoons soy sauce in shallow dish; let stand 5 minutes. Combine flour and black pepper on plate. Gently toss tofu cubes, a small amount at a time, with flour mixture to coat. Spray tofu with nonstick cooking spray.

2 Preheat air fryer to 390°F. Cook in batches 3 to 4 minutes or until browned. Remove to plate; keep warm.

3 Place frozen vegetables in basket. Cook 3 to 4 minutes, shaking halfway through cooking, until vegetables are heated through. Set aside; cover to keep warm.

4 Stir water into cornstarch in small bowl until well blended. Combine cornstarch mixture, remaining 2 tablespoons soy sauce, plum sauce, lemon juice, sugar, ginger and red pepper flakes in medium microwavable bowl; cover and heat in microwave on HIGH 1 minute or until sauce is slightly thickened; stir to mix well. Spoon vegetables into serving bowl. Top with tofu and sauce; toss gently to mix.

MAKES 6 SERVINGS

CALORIES 190 · TOTAL FAT 4.5g · SATURATED FAT 0g · CHOLESTEROL 0mg
SODIUM 860mg · CARBOHYDRATE 25g · DIETARY FIBER 0g · PROTEIN 12g

AIR-FRIED TURKEY BREAST WITH ROASTED SQUASH

4 cups water

¼ cup coarse salt

⅓ cup packed brown sugar

1 frozen turkey breast roast (3 pounds), thawed

3 tablespoons melted butter

Salt and pepper

2 medium zucchini *or* 1 medium zucchini and 1 medium yellow squash, cut into slices

1 tablespoon olive oil

1 Combine water, coarse salt and brown sugar in medium saucepan. Bring to a boil. Remove from heat; stir and let cool about 20 to 30 minutes or until room temperature.

2 Remove packaging from turkey breast, leaving netting in place. Place in large resealable food storage bag. Pour liquid over turkey; seal and place in large bowl. Refrigerate 6 hours or overnight.

3 Preheat air fryer to 390°F. Remove turkey from liquid, discarding liquid. Dry turkey with paper towels. Brush with half of butter.

4 Cook turkey, with netting in place, 15 minutes, turning halfway through cooking. Remove netting. Reduce temperature to 350°F. Brush turkey with remaining butter; cook 15 minutes. Turn, cook 12 to 15 minutes or until turkey reaches internal temperature of 165°F. Remove turkey; let stand 10 minutes.

5 Slice turkey. Season with salt and pepper.

6 Meanwhile, toss zucchini with oil. Set air fryer to 370°F. Cook 10 to 12 minutes or until tender and browned. Serve with turkey.

MAKES 8 SERVINGS

CALORIES 260 · TOTAL FAT 8g · SATURATED FAT 3.5g · CHOLESTEROL 100mg
SODIUM 150mg · CARBOHYDRATE 3g · DIETARY FIBER 0g · PROTEIN 37g

FRIED TOFU WITH SESAME DIPPING SAUCE

3 tablespoons soy sauce or tamari

2 tablespoons unseasoned rice vinegar

2 teaspoons sugar

1 teaspoon sesame seeds, toasted*

1 teaspoon dark sesame oil

⅛ teaspoon red pepper flakes

1 package (about 14 ounces) extra firm tofu

¼ cup all-purpose flour

1 egg

1 cup panko bread crumbs

Salt

To toast sesame seeds, spread seeds in small skillet. Shake skillet over medium-low heat about 3 minutes or until seeds begin to pop and turn golden.

1 Whisk soy sauce, vinegar, sugar, sesame seeds, sesame oil and red pepper flakes in small bowl until well blended; set aside.

2 Drain tofu and press between paper towels to remove excess water. Cut crosswise into four slices; cut each slice diagonally into triangles. Place flour in shallow dish. Beat egg in shallow bowl. Place panko in another shallow bowl.

3 Dip each piece of tofu in flour, turning to lightly coat all sides. Dip in egg, letting excess drip back into bowl. Roll in panko to coat. Season with salt.

4 Preheat air fryer to 390°F. Spray tofu with nonstick cooking spray. Cook in batches 5 to 6 minutes or until golden brown. Serve with sauce for dipping.

MAKES 4 SERVINGS

CALORIES 250 · TOTAL FAT 9g · SATURATED FAT 1g · CHOLESTEROL 45mg
SODIUM 930mg · CARBOHYDRATE 25g · DIETARY FIBER 0g · PROTEIN 17g

CHICKEN WITH HERB STUFFING

⅓ **cup fresh basil leaves**

1 **package (8 ounces) goat cheese with garlic and herbs**

4 **boneless skinless chicken breasts**

1 **tablespoon olive oil**

1 Place basil in food processor; process using on/off pulsing action until chopped. Cut goat cheese into large pieces and add to food processor; process using on/off pulsing action until combined.

2 Place 1 chicken breast on cutting board and cover with plastic wrap. Pound with meat mallet until ¼ inch thick. Repeat with remaining chicken.

3 Shape about 2 tablespoons of cheese mixture into log and set in center of each chicken breast. Wrap chicken around filling to enclose completely. Tie securely with kitchen string. Drizzle with oil.

4 Preheat air fryer to 370°F. Cook 15 to 20 minutes or until chicken is cooked through and filling is hot. Allow to cool slightly, remove string and slice to serve.

MAKES 4 SERVINGS

CALORIES 330 · TOTAL FAT 21g · SATURATED FAT 9g · CHOLESTEROL 145mg
SODIUM 270mg · CARBOHYDRATE 2g · DIETARY FIBER 0g · PROTEIN 36g

ROASTED ALMOND TILAPIA

2   **tilapia or Boston scrod fillets
    (4 ounces each)**

⅛   **teaspoon salt**

2   **teaspoons mustard**

¼   **cup all-purpose flour**

2   **tablespoons chopped almonds**

    Paprika (optional)

    Lemon wedges (optional)

1   Season fish with salt. Spread mustard over fish. Combine flour and almonds in small bowl; sprinkle over fish. Press lightly to adhere. Sprinkle with paprika, if desired.

2   Preheat air fryer to 370°F. Line basket with parchment paper.

3   Cook in batches 12 to 15 minutes or until fish is opaque in center and begins to easily flake when tested with a fork. Serve with lemon wedges, if desired.

MAKES 2 SERVINGS

CALORIES 180 · TOTAL FAT 5g · SATURATED FAT 0g · CHOLESTEROL 55mg
SODIUM 270mg · CARBOHYDRATE 9g · DIETARY FIBER 1g · PROTEIN 26g

LEMON-PEPPER CHICKEN

⅓ **cup lemon juice**

¼ **cup finely chopped onion**

2 **tablespoons olive oil**

1 **tablespoon packed brown sugar**

1 **tablespoon black pepper**

3 **cloves garlic, minced**

2 **teaspoons grated lemon peel**

½ **teaspoon salt**

4 **boneless skinless chicken breasts (about 1 pound)**

1 Combine lemon juice, onion, oil, brown sugar, pepper, garlic, lemon peel and salt in small bowl; stir to blend. Pour marinade over chicken in large resealable food storage bag. Seal bag; knead to coat. Refrigerate at least 4 hours or overnight.

2 Preheat air fryer to 370°F. Line basket with parchment paper or foil; spray with nonstick cooking spray.

3 Remove chicken from marinade; discard marinade. Cook in batches 15 to 20 minutes or until chicken is browned and no longer pink in center.

MAKES 4 SERVINGS

LEMON-PEPPER CHICKEN ON MIXED GREENS:
Toss 4 cups spring greens; 1 cup grape tomatoes, halved; and ½ cup sliced red onion in large bowl. Top with Lemon-Pepper Chicken breast. Serve with herb viniagrette or your favorite salad dressing.

CALORIES 220 · TOTAL FAT 10g · SATURATED FAT 1.5g · CHOLESTEROL 85mg
SODIUM 350mg · CARBOHYDRATE 7g · DIETARY FIBER 1g · PROTEIN 26g

SALMON-POTATO CAKES WITH MUSTARD TARTAR SAUCE

3 small unpeeled red potatoes (8 ounces), halved

1 cup water

1 cup flaked cooked salmon

2 green onions, chopped

1 egg white

2 tablespoons chopped fresh parsley, divided

½ teaspoon Cajun or Creole seasoning

1 tablespoon light mayonnaise

1 tablespoon plain nonfat yogurt or fat-free sour cream

2 teaspoons coarse grain mustard

1 tablespoon chopped dill pickle

1 teaspoon lemon juice

1 Place potatoes and water in medium saucepan. Bring to a boil. Reduce heat and simmer about 15 minutes or until potatoes are tender. Drain. Mash potatoes with fork, leaving chunky texture.

2 Combine mashed potatoes, salmon, green onions, egg white, 1 tablespoon parsley and Cajun seasoning in medium bowl.

3 Preheat air fryer to 370°F. Gently shape salmon mixture into patties; flatten slightly. Cook 5 to 6 minutes, flipping halfway through cooking, until browned and heated through.

4 Meanwhile, combine mayonnaise, yogurt, mustard, remaining 1 tablespoon parsley, pickle and lemon juice in small bowl. Serve sauce with cakes.

MAKES 4 SERVINGS

CALORIES 200 · TOTAL FAT 4.5g · SATURATED FAT 1g · CHOLESTEROL 20mg
SODIUM 300mg · CARBOHYDRATE 27g · DIETARY FIBER 3g · PROTEIN 12g

BANG-BANG CHICKEN ON RICE

CREAMY HOT SAUCE

- ½ cup mayonnaise
- ¼ cup sweet chili sauce
- 1½ teaspoons hot pepper sauce

CHICKEN

- 1 pound chicken breasts, cut into 1-inch pieces
- ¾ cup panko bread crumbs
- ½ cup all-purpose flour
- 2 cups hot cooked rice
- 2 green onions, chopped

1 Prepare Creamy Hot Sauce. Combine mayonnaise, chili sauce and hot pepper sauce in medium bowl. Divide mixture in half; set one half aside.

2 Put chicken in large bowl. Place panko in shallow dish.

3 Using hands, mix toss chicken with flour until well coated. Dip chicken pieces in Creamy Hot Sauce, then coat in panko. Spray with nonstick cooking spray.

4 Preheat air fryer to 390°F. Line basket with parchment paper.

5 Cook chicken in batches 10 to 12 minutes until golden brown. Remove chicken to large bowl; toss with remaining Creamy Hot Sauce.

6 Serve over rice. Sprinkle with green onions.

MAKES 4 SERVINGS

CALORIES 460 · TOTAL FAT 23g · SATURATED FAT 3.5g · CHOLESTEROL 95mg
SODIUM 380mg · CARBOHYDRATE 32g · DIETARY FIBER 1g · PROTEIN 29g

BALSAMIC CHICKEN

1½ **teaspoons fresh rosemary leaves, minced, *or* ½ teaspoon dried rosemary**

2 **cloves garlic, minced**

¾ **teaspoon black pepper**

½ **teaspoon salt**

6 **boneless skinless chicken breasts (about ¼ pound each)**

1 **tablespoon olive oil**

¼ **cup balsamic vinegar**

1 Combine rosemary, garlic, pepper and salt in small bowl; mix well. Place chicken in large bowl; drizzle chicken with oil and rub with spice mixture. Cover and refrigerate several hours.

2 Preheat air fryer to 390°F. Spray basket with nonstick cooking spray.

3 Cook in batches 10 to 12 minutes or until chicken is no longer pink in center. Remove to plates.

4 Drizzle vinegar over chicken.

MAKES 6 SERVINGS

CALORIES 160 · TOTAL FAT 5g · SATURATED FAT 1g · CHOLESTEROL 85mg
SODIUM 250mg · CARBOHYDRATE 1g · DIETARY FIBER 0g · PROTEIN 26g

LEMON-PEPPER SHRIMP ON GARLIC SPINACH

2½ teaspoons olive oil, divided

3 tablespoons lemon juice, divided

½ teaspoon ground black pepper

¼ teaspoon paprika

¼ teaspoon garlic powder

1 pound uncooked medium shrimp, peeled and deveined

2 cloves garlic, minced

8 ounces fresh baby spinach leaves (about 8 cups lightly packed), washed

¼ cup water

1 Combine 1½ teaspoons oil, 1 tablespoon lemon juice, pepper, paprika and garlic powder in medium bowl. Add shrimp; toss to coat.

2 Preheat air fryer to 390°F. Spray basket with nonstick cooking spray.

3 Cook 6 to 8 minutes or until shrimp are firm and no longer pink.

4 Meanwhile, heat remaining 1 teaspoon oil in small skillet over medium-high heat. Add garlic; cook 1 minute. Add spinach and water. Cook 4 to 5 minutes or until spinach is wilted. Drain; keep warm.

5 Serve shrimp over spinach.

MAKES 4 SERVINGS

CALORIES 130 · TOTAL FAT 4g · SATURATED FAT 0.5g · CHOLESTEROL 145mg
SODIUM 690mg · CARBOHYDRATE 5g · DIETARY FIBER 2g · PROTEIN 17g

BAKED PANKO CHICKEN

½ cup panko bread crumbs

3 teaspoons assorted dried herbs (such as rosemary, basil, parsley, thyme or oregano), divided

Salt and black pepper

2 tablespoons mayonnaise

2 boneless skinless chicken breasts

1 Combine panko, 1 teaspoon herbs, salt and pepper in shallow dish. Combine mayonnaise and remaining 2 teaspoons herbs in small bowl. Spread mayonnaise mixture onto chicken. Coat chicken with panko mixture, pressing to adhere.

2 Preheat air fryer to 390°F. Line basket with parchment paper; spray with nonstick cooking spray.

3 Cook 18 to 20 minutes or until chicken is browned and no longer pink in center.

MAKES 2 SERVINGS

CALORIES 300 · TOTAL FAT 13g · SATURATED FAT 2.5g · CHOLESTEROL 90mg
SODIUM 170mg · CARBOHYDRATE 15g · DIETARY FIBER 0g · PROTEIN 28g

SALMON NUGGETS WITH BROCCOLI

1 **pound skinless salmon fillet**

2 **eggs**

1 **cup plain dry bread crumbs**

1½ **teaspoons salt, divided**

2 **cups broccoli florets**

1 **tablespoon olive oil**

Sweet and sour sauce or other favorite dipping sauce (optional)

1 Cut salmon into 1-inch chunks.

2 Whisk eggs in small bowl. Combine bread crumbs and 1 teaspoon salt in shallow dish. Dip salmon chunks in egg, letting excess drip back in dish. Coat evenly with bread crumbs. Set on plate; spray lightly with nonstick cooking spray.

3 Preheat air fryer to 390°F. Spray basket with cooking spray.

4 Cook in batches 3 to 4 minutes; flip nuggets over. Spray with cooking spray. Cook 3 to 4 minutes until golden brown.

5 Meanwhile, toss broccoli with oil in large bowl. Sprinkle with remaining ½ teaspoon salt. Cook broccoli 6 to 8 minutes or until browned and crispy.

6 Serve nuggets and broccoli with sweet and sour sauce or other dipping sauce, if desired.

MAKES 5 SERVINGS

SUBSTITUTE: Try garlic-herb bread crumbs or Italian-seasoned instead of plain.

CALORIES 330 · TOTAL FAT 18g · SATURATED FAT 4g · CHOLESTEROL 125mg
SODIUM 600mg · CARBOHYDRATE 17g · DIETARY FIBER 2g · PROTEIN 25g

ROAST DILL SCROD WITH ASPARAGUS

1 bunch (12 ounces) asparagus spears, ends trimmed

1 teaspoon olive oil

4 scrod or cod fillets (about 5 ounces each)

1 tablespoon lemon juice

1 teaspoon dried dill weed

½ teaspoon salt

¼ teaspoon black pepper

Paprika (optional)

1   Preheat air fryer to 390°F. Line basket with parchment paper.

2   Drizzle asparagus with oil. Roll asparagus to coat lightly with oil. Cook 8 to 10 minutes or until tender. Remove; keep warm.

3   Drizzle fish with lemon juice. Combine dill weed, salt and pepper in small bowl; sprinkle over fish.

4   Cook 10 to 12 minutes or until fish is opaque in center and begins to flake when tested with a fork. Place fish and asparagus on serving plate. Sprinkle with paprika, if desired.

MAKES 4 SERVINGS

CALORIES 150 · TOTAL FAT 2g · SATURATED FAT 0g · CHOLESTEROL 60mg
SODIUM 370mg · CARBOHYDRATE 4g · DIETARY FIBER 2g · PROTEIN 27g

EASY AIR-FRIED CHICKEN THIGHS

8 bone-in or boneless chicken thighs with skin (about 1½ pounds)

½ **teaspoon garlic powder**

½ **teaspoon onion powder**

½ **teaspoon dried oregano**

½ **teaspoon ground thyme**

½ **teaspoon paprika**

¼ **teaspoon salt**

½ **teaspoon black pepper**

1 Place chicken in large resealable food storage bag. Combine garlic powder, onion powder, oregano, thyme, paprika, salt and pepper in small bowl; mix well. Add to chicken; shake until spices are distributed.

2 Preheat air fryer to 350°F. Line basket with parchment paper; spray with nonstick cooking spray.

3 Cook in batches 20 to 25 minutes until golden brown and cooked through, turning chicken halfway through cooking.

MAKES 4 SERVINGS

CALORIES 130 · TOTAL FAT 5g · SATURATED FAT 1g · CHOLESTEROL 95mg
SODIUM 250mg · CARBOHYDRATE 1g · DIETARY FIBER 0g · PROTEIN 20g

TUNA CAKES WITH CREAMY CUCUMBER SAUCE

½ **cup finely chopped cucumber**

6 **ounces fat-free plain yogurt or fat-free plain Greek yogurt**

1½ **teaspoons chopped fresh dill** *or* **½ teaspoon dried dill weed**

1 **teaspoon lemon-pepper seasoning**

⅓ **cup shredded carrots**

¼ **cup sliced green onions**

¼ **cup finely chopped celery**

¼ **cup mayonnaise**

2 **teaspoons spicy brown mustard**

1 **cup panko bread crumbs, divided**

1 **can (12 ounces) albacore tuna in water, drained**

Lemon wedges (optional)

1 For sauce, stir together cucumber, yogurt, dill and lemon-pepper seasoning in small bowl. Cover and refrigerate until serving time.

2 In mixing bowl, combine carrots, green onions, celery, mayonnaise and mustard. Stir in ½ cup panko. Add tuna and mix until combined.

3 Place remaining ½ cup panko in shallow dish. Shape tuna mixture into five (½-inch-thick) patties. Dip patties in panko, lightly coating.

4 Preheat air fryer to 370°F. Spray basket with nonstick cooking spray.

5 Cook in batches 6 to 8 minutes, flipping halfway during cooking, until golden brown. Serve with yogurt mixture and garnish with lemon wedges.

MAKES 5 SERVINGS

CALORIES 200 · TOTAL FAT 5g · SATURATED FAT 0.5g · CHOLESTEROL 35mg
SODIUM 320mg · CARBOHYDRATE 16g · DIETARY FIBER 0g · PROTEIN 21g

CAULIFLOWER TACOS WITH CHIPOTLE CREMA

1 **package (8 ounces) sliced cremini mushrooms**

4 **tablespoons olive oil, divided**

¼ **teaspoon salt**

1 **head cauliflower**

1 **teaspoon ground cumin**

½ **teaspoon dried oregano**

¼ **teaspoon ground coriander**

¼ **teaspoon ground cinnamon**

¼ **teaspoon black pepper**

½ **cup reduced-fat sour cream**

2 **teaspoons lime juice**

½ **teaspoon chipotle chili powder**

½ **cup vegetarian refried beans**

8 **(6-inch) corn or flour tortillas**

Chopped fresh cilantro (optional)

Pickled Red Onions (recipe follows) or chopped red onion

1 Toss mushrooms with 1 tablespoon oil and salt in large bowl.

2 Remove leaves from cauliflower. Cut florets into 1-inch pieces; place in large bowl. Add remaining 3 tablespoons oil, cumin, oregano, coriander, cinnamon and pepper; toss well.

3 Preheat air fryer to 390°F. Spray basket with nonstick cooking spray. Cook cauliflower in batches 8 to 10 minutes or until browned and tender, shaking occasionally. Remove to large bowl.

4 Add mushrooms to basket. Cook 6 to 8 minutes or until browned, shaking occasionally.

5 For crema, combine sour cream, lime juice and chili powder in small bowl.

6 For each taco, spread 1 tablespoon beans and 1 teaspoon crema over each tortilla. Top with about 3 mushroom slices and ¼ cup cauliflower. Top with cilantro and red onions, if desired. Fold in half.

MAKES 8 TACOS

PICKLED RED ONIONS: Thinly slice 1 small red onion; place in large glass jar. Add ¼ cup white wine vinegar or distilled white vinegar, 2 tablespoons water, 1 teaspoon sugar and 1 teaspoon salt. Seal jar; shake well. Refrigerate at least 1 hour or up to 1 week. Makes about ½ cup.

CALORIES 180 · TOTAL FAT 10g · SATURATED FAT 2g · CHOLESTEROL 10mg
SODIUM 150mg · CARBOHYDRATE 20g · DIETARY FIBER 3g · PROTEIN 5g

GARLICKY AIR-FRIED CHICKEN THIGHS

1 egg

2 tablespoons water

1 cup plain dry bread crumbs

1 teaspoon salt

1 teaspoon garlic powder

½ teaspoon black pepper

¼ teaspoon ground red pepper

8 chicken thighs (about 3 pounds)

1 Beat egg and water in shallow dish. Combine bread crumbs, salt, garlic powder, black pepper and ground red pepper in separate shallow dish.

2 Dip chicken into egg mixture; turn to coat. Transfer to bread crumb mixture; press lightly to coat both sides.

3 Preheat air fryer to 390°F.

4 Lightly spray chicken with nonstick cooking spray. Cook 20 to 22 minutes or until browned and cooked through.

MAKES 4 SERVINGS

VARIATIONS: Substitute seasoned bread crumbs for the plain bread crumbs, garlic powder, ground red pepper, salt and black pepper. Or, substitute your favorite dried herbs or spices for the garlic powder and ground red pepper; thyme, sage, oregano or rosemary would be delicious, as would Cajun or Creole seasoning.

CALORIES 380 · TOTAL FAT 11g · SATURATED FAT 3g · CHOLESTEROL 240mg
SODIUM 700mg · CARBOHYDRATE 20g · DIETARY FIBER 0g · PROTEIN 45g

RICOTTA AND SPINACH HASSELBACK CHICKEN

½ **cup fresh baby spinach leaves**

1 **teaspoon olive oil**

2 **tablespoons reduced-fat ricotta cheese**

2 **boneless skinless chicken breasts (about 4 ounces each)**

⅛ **teaspoon salt**

⅛ **teaspoon black pepper**

2 **tablespoons shredded reduced-fat Cheddar cheese**

1 Place spinach and oil in small microwavable dish. Microwave on HIGH 20 to 30 seconds or until spinach is slightly wilted. Stir ricotta cheese into spinach; mix well.

2 Cut four diagonal slits three fourths of the way into each chicken breast (do not cut all the way through). Place about 1 teaspoon ricotta mixture into each slit. Sprinkle chicken with salt and pepper.

3 Preheat air fryer to 390°F. Line basket with foil.

4 Cook 12 minutes. Top chicken with Cheddar cheese.

5 Cook 4 to 6 minutes or until cheese melts, chicken is golden and juices run clear.

MAKES 2 SERVINGS

CALORIES 180 · TOTAL FAT 7g · SATURATED FAT 3g · CHOLESTEROL 65mg
SODIUM 520mg · CARBOHYDRATE 2g · DIETARY FIBER 0g · PROTEIN 26g

CHICKEN PICCATA

3 tablespoons all-purpose flour

½ teaspoon salt

¼ teaspoon black pepper

4 boneless skinless chicken breasts (4 ounces each)

1 teaspoon butter

2 cloves garlic, minced

¾ cup fat-free reduced-sodium chicken broth

1 tablespoon fresh lemon juice

2 tablespoons chopped fresh Italian parsley

1 tablespoon capers, drained

1 Combine flour, salt and pepper in shallow dish. Reserve 1 tablespoon flour mixture for sauce.

2 Pound chicken to ½-inch thickness between sheets of waxed paper with flat side of meat mallet or rolling pin. Coat chicken with remaining flour mixture, shaking off excess. Spray with nonstick cooking spray.

3 Preheat air fryer to 370°F. Line basket with parchment paper. Cook 15 to 20 minutes or until chicken is browned and no longer pink in center.

4 Heat butter and garlic in nonstick skillet over medium heat; cook and stir 1 minute. Add reserved flour mixture; cook and stir 1 minute. Add broth and lemon juice; cook 2 minutes or until sauce thickens, stirring frequently. Stir in parsley and capers; spoon sauce over chicken.

MAKES 4 SERVINGS

CALORIES 170 · TOTAL FAT 4g · SATURATED FAT 1.5g · CHOLESTEROL 85mg
SODIUM 460mg · CARBOHYDRATE 6g · DIETARY FIBER 0g · PROTEIN 27g

EASY TERIYAKI BURGERS

1 **pound lean ground beef**

½ **cup plain dry bread crumbs**

¼ **cup low-sodium ketchup**

2 **tablespoons low-sodium teriyaki sauce**

½ **teaspoon black pepper**

6 **Kaiser rolls or hamburger buns, warmed**

6 **leaves green leaf lettuce**

6 **slices tomato**

1 Combine beef, bread crumbs, ketchup, teriyaki sauce and pepper in large bowl; mix well. Shape beef into four (½-inch-thick) patties.

2 Preheat air fryer to 370°F.

3 Cook in batches 8 to 10 minutes, flipping halfway through cooking, until desired doneness. Place patties on rolls. Serve with lettuce and tomato slices.

MAKES 6 SERVINGS

CALORIES 280 · TOTAL FAT 6g · SATURATED FAT 2g · CHOLESTEROL 45mg
SODIUM 400mg · CARBOHYDRATE 29g · DIETARY FIBER 3g · PROTEIN 23g

BREADED VEAL SCALLOPINI WITH MUSHROOMS

½ **pound veal cutlets**

¼ **teaspoon salt**

⅛ **teaspoon black pepper**

1 **egg**

1 **tablespoon water**

½ **cup plain dry bread crumbs**

1 **tablespoon unsalted butter**

2 **large shallots, chopped (about ¼ cup)**

8 **ounces exotic mushrooms, such as cremini, oyster, baby bella and shiitake***

½ **teaspoon herbes de Provence****

½ **cup reduced-sodium chicken broth**

2 **lemon wedges (optional)**

Exotic mushrooms make this dish special. However, you can substitute white button mushrooms, if you prefer.

**Herbes de Provence is a mixture of basil, fennel, lavender, marjoram, rosemary, sage, savory and thyme used to season meat, poultry and vegetables.*

1 Season cutlets with salt and pepper. Lightly beat egg with water in shallow dish. Place bread crumbs in separate shallow dish.

2 Dip cutlet into egg, letting excess drip off. Dip in bread crumbs, turning to coat. Repeat with remaining cutlets.

3 Preheat air fryer to 370°F. Spray basket with nonstick cooking spray. Cook 12 to 15 minutes, turning halfway, until golden brown and cooked through. Transfer to plate.

4 Heat butter in large skillet over medium-high heat. Add shallots; cook and stir 1 to 2 minutes or until translucent. Add mushrooms and herbes de Provence; cook and stir 3 to 4 minutes or until most of liquid is evaporated. Stir in broth; cook 2 to 3 minutes or until slightly thickened.

5 Pour mushroom mixture over cutlets. Garnish with lemon wedges.

MAKES 2 SERVINGS

CALORIES 450 · TOTAL FAT 22g · SATURATED FAT 10g · CHOLESTEROL 195mg
SODIUM 720mg · CARBOHYDRATE 29g · DIETARY FIBER 1g · PROTEIN 33g

TERIYAKI SALMON

¼ **cup dark sesame oil**

Juice of 1 lemon

¼ **cup soy sauce**

2 **tablespoons packed brown sugar**

1 **clove garlic, minced**

2 **salmon fillets (about 4 ounces each)**

Hot cooked rice

Toasted sesame seeds and green onions (optional)

1 Whisk oil, lemon juice, soy sauce, brown sugar and garlic in medium bowl. Place salmon in large resealable food storage bag; add marinade. Refrigerate at least 2 hours.

2 Preheat air fryer to 350°F. Spray basket with nonstick cooking spray.

3 Cook 8 to 10 minutes until salmon is crispy and easily flakes when tested with a fork. Serve with rice and garnish as desired.

MAKES 2 SERVINGS

CALORIES 320 · TOTAL FAT 22g · SATURATED FAT 4.5g · CHOLESTEROL 60mg
SODIUM 650mg · CARBOHYDRATE 4g · DIETARY FIBER 0g · PROTEIN 24g

BREADED PORK CUTLETS WITH TONKATSU SAUCE

Tonkatsu Sauce (recipe follows)

½ cup all-purpose flour

2 eggs, beaten with 2 tablespoons water

1½ cups panko bread crumbs

1 pound pork tenderloin, trimmed of fat and sliced into ½-inch-thick pieces

2 cups hot cooked rice

1 Prepare Tonkatsu Sauce; set aside.

2 Place flour in shallow dish. Place eggs in another shallow dish. Spread panko on medium plate. Dip each pork slice first in flour, then egg. Shake off excess and coat in panko.

3 Preheat air fryer to 370°F. Cook 12 to 15 minutes or until cooked through.

4 Serve over rice with Tonkatsu Sauce.

MAKES 4 SERVINGS

TONKATSU SAUCE

¼ cup ketchup

1 tablespoon soy sauce

2 teaspoons sugar

2 teaspoons mirin (Japanese sweet rice wine)

1 teaspoon Worcestershire sauce

½ teaspoon grated fresh ginger

1 clove garlic, minced

Combine ketchup, soy sauce, sugar, mirin, Worcestershire sauce, ginger and garlic in small bowl.

MAKES ABOUT ⅓ CUP SAUCE

CALORIES 420 · TOTAL FAT 5g · SATURATED FAT 1.5g · CHOLESTEROL 160mg
SODIUM 290mg · CARBOHYDRATE 57g · DIETARY FIBER 1g · PROTEIN 33g

CHICKEN WITH KALE STUFFING

4 **boneless skinless chicken breasts**

1 **cup sliced mushrooms**

½ **cup chopped onion**

2 **tablespoons dry white wine**

1 **teaspoon chopped fresh oregano** *or* ¼ **teaspoon dried oregano**

1 **clove garlic, minced**

½ **teaspoon black pepper**

2 **cups packed chopped stemmed kale**

2 **tablespoons light mayonnaise**

½ **cup seasoned dry bread crumbs**

1 Pound chicken with meat mallet to ½-inch thickness; set aside.

2 Heat skillet over medium-high heat. Add mushrooms, onion, wine, oregano, garlic and pepper; cook and stir about 5 minutes or until onion is tender. Add kale; cook and stir until wilted.

3 Spread kale mixture evenly over flattened chicken breasts. Roll up chicken; secure with toothpicks. Brush chicken with mayonnaise; coat with bread crumbs.

4 Preheat air fryer to 370°F. Spray basket with nonstick cooking spray.

5 Cook chicken, seam sides down, 15 to 20 minutes or until chicken is golden brown and no longer pink in center. Remove toothpicks before serving.

MAKES 4 SERVINGS

CALORIES 240 • TOTAL FAT 6g • SATURATED FAT 1g • CHOLESTEROL 85mg
SODIUM 200mg • CARBOHYDRATE 14g • DIETARY FIBER 1g • PROTEIN 29g

BEER AIR-FRIED CHICKEN

1⅓ cups light-colored beer, such as pale ale

2 tablespoons buttermilk

1¼ cups panko bread crumbs

½ cup grated Parmesan cheese

4 chicken breast cutlets (about 1¼ pounds)

½ teaspoon salt

¼ teaspoon black pepper

1 Combine beer and buttermilk in shallow dish. Combine panko and Parmesan cheese in another shallow dish.

2 Sprinkle chicken with salt and pepper. Dip in beer mixture; roll in panko mixture to coat.

3 Preheat air fryer to 370°F. Line basket with foil; spray with nonstick cooking spray.

4 Cook in batches 18 to 20 minutes or until chicken is no longer pink in center.

MAKES 4 SERVINGS

TIP: To make a substitution for buttermilk, place 1 teaspoon lemon juice or distilled white vinegar in a measuring cup and add enough milk to measure ⅓ cup. Stir and let the mixture stand at room temperature for 5 minutes. Discard leftover mixture.

CALORIES 330 · TOTAL FAT 6g · SATURATED FAT 3g · CHOLESTEROL 95mg
SODIUM 670mg · CARBOHYDRATE 22g · DIETARY FIBER 0g · PROTEIN 42g

SIDES & FRIES

AIR-ROASTED SWEET POTATOES

2 sweet potatoes, peeled and cut into thin or spiral slices

1 tablespoon olive oil

Pinch salt

Ground black pepper

¼ cup grated Parmesan cheese (optional)

1 Preheat air fryer to 330°F.

2 Toss sweet potatoes and oil in medium bowl. Season with salt and pepper.

3 Cook in batches 20 to 22 minutes, shaking halfway through cooking.

4 Sprinkle with cheese, if desired.

MAKES 4 SERVINGS

CALORIES 80 • TOTAL FAT 3.5g • SATURATED FAT 0g • CHOLESTEROL 0mg
SODIUM 35mg • CARBOHYDRATE 12g • DIETARY FIBER 2g • PROTEIN 1g

ROASTED ASPARAGUS

1 **bunch (14 ounces) asparagus spears**

1 **tablespoon olive oil**

½ **teaspoon salt**

¼ **teaspoon black pepper**

¼ **cup shredded Asiago or Parmesan cheese (optional)**

1 Trim off and discard tough ends of asparagus spears. Peel stem ends with vegetable peeler, if desired. Arrange asparagus in shallow baking dish; drizzle with oil, turning spears to coat. Sprinkle with salt and pepper.

2 Preheat air fryer to 390°F.

3 Cook in batches 8 to 10 minutes, shaking occasionally during cooking, until tender. Sprinkle with cheese, if desired.

MAKES 4 SERVINGS

CALORIES 50 • TOTAL FAT 3.5g • SATURATED FAT 0.5g • CHOLESTEROL 0mg
SODIUM 300mg • CARBOHYDRATE 4g • DIETARY FIBER 2g • PROTEIN 2g

GARLIC-HERB PARMESAN DIPPING STICKS

1 **package (about 14 ounces) refrigerated pizza dough**

¾ **cup light garlic-and-herb spreadable cheese**

¾ **cup (3 ounces) shredded Italian cheese blend**

¼ **cup grated Parmesan cheese**

½ **teaspoon dried oregano**

Warm marinara sauce and/ or ranch salad dressing (optional)

1 Roll out dough on lightly floured surface to 12-inch square. Spread garlic-and-herb spreadable cheese evenly over bread. Top with cheese blend, Parmesan cheese and oregano.

2 Preheat air fryer to 390°F. Line basket with parchment paper; spray with nonstick cooking spray.

3 Cut dough in half or thirds to fit into basket. Cook in batches 6 to 8 minutes or until golden brown. Let cool slightly.

4 Slice lengthwise into strips. Serve with marinara sauce or salad dressing for dipping, if desired.

MAKES 12 SERVINGS

CALORIES 135 · TOTAL FAT 5g · SATURATED FAT 3g · CHOLESTEROL 11mg
SODIUM 404mg · CARBOHYDRATE 17g · DIETARY FIBER 1g · PROTEIN 6g

ROASTED POTATOES AND ONIONS WITH HERBS

2 **pounds unpeeled red potatoes, cut into 1½-inch pieces**

1 **sweet onion, such as Vidalia or Walla Walla, coarsely chopped**

2 **tablespoons olive oil**

2 **cloves garlic, minced**

½ **teaspoon salt**

¼ **teaspoon black pepper**

¼ **cup packed chopped mixed fresh herbs, such as basil, chives, parsley, oregano, rosemary leaves, sage, tarragon and thyme**

1 Place potatoes and onion in large bowl. Combine oil, garlic, salt and pepper in small bowl. Drizzle over potatoes and onion; toss well to coat.

2 Preheat air fryer to 390°F. Line basket with foil.

3 Cook 18 to 20 minutes, shaking occasionally during cooking, until potatoes are tender and browned. Remove to large bowl. Add herbs; toss well.

MAKES 6 SERVINGS

CALORIES 160 · TOTAL FAT 5g · SATURATED FAT 0.5g · CHOLESTEROL 0mg
SODIUM 230mg · CARBOHYDRATE 27g · DIETARY FIBER 3g · PROTEIN 3g

AIR-FRIED CORN-ON-THE-COB

2 teaspoons butter, melted

¼ teaspoon salt

½ teaspoon black pepper

½ teaspoon chopped fresh parsley

2 ears corn, husks and silks removed

Foil

Grated Parmesan cheese (optional)

1 Combine butter, salt, pepper and parsley in small bowl. Brush corn with butter mixture. Wrap each ear of corn in foil.*

2 Preheat air fryer to 390°F. Cook 10 to 12 minutes, turning halfway through cooking. Sprinkle with Parmesan cheese before serving, if desired.

If your air fryer basket is on the smaller side, you may need to break ears of corn in half to fit.

MAKES 2 SERVINGS

CALORIES 110 · TOTAL FAT 5g · SATURATED FAT 2.5g · CHOLESTEROL 10mg
SODIUM 310mg · CARBOHYDRATE 17g · DIETARY FIBER 3g · PROTEIN 3g

HASSELBACK POTATOES

4 small Yukon Gold potatoes

3 tablespoons butter, melted and divided

½ teaspoon salt

¼ teaspoon ground black pepper

¼ cup grated Parmesan cheese

Chopped fresh parsley

1 Preheat air fryer to 390°F.

2 Cut diagonal slits into each potato about ⅛ inch apart and ¾ inch down (do not cut all the way through). Brush 2 tablespoons butter over tops; sprinkle with salt and pepper.

3 Cook 20 to 22 minutes or until slightly softened and lightly browned.

4 Brush potatoes with remaining 1 tablespoon butter. Sprinkle with Parmesan cheese. Cook 3 to 5 minutes. Sprinkle with parsley.

MAKES 4 SERVINGS

CALORIES 230 · TOTAL FAT 11g · SATURATED FAT 7g · CHOLESTEROL 30mg
SODIUM 420mg · CARBOHYDRATE 29g · DIETARY FIBER 3g · PROTEIN 7g

CORNMEAL-CRUSTED CAULIFLOWER STEAKS

½ cup cornmeal

¼ cup all-purpose flour

1 teaspoon salt

1 teaspoon dried sage

½ teaspoon garlic powder

Black pepper

½ cup milk

2 heads cauliflower

2 tablespoons butter, melted

Barbecue sauce (optional)

1 Combine cornmeal, flour, salt, sage, garlic powder and pepper in shallow dish. Pour milk into another shallow dish.

2 Turn cauliflower stem side up on cutting board. Trim away leaves, leaving stem intact. Slice through stem into 2 or 3 slices. Trim off excess florets from two end slices, creating flat "steaks." Repeat with remaining cauliflower; reserve extra cauliflower for another use.

3 Dip cauliflower into milk to coat both sides. Place in cornmeal mixture; pat onto all sides of cauliflower. Drizzle butter evenly over cauliflower.

4 Preheat air fryer to 390°F. Line basket with parchment paper.

5 Cook in batches 12 to 15 minutes, flipping halfway through cooking, until cauliflower is tender. Serve with barbecue sauce for dipping, if desired.

MAKES 4 SERVINGS

CALORIES 190 · TOTAL FAT 7g · SATURATED FAT 4g · CHOLESTEROL 20mg
SODIUM 880mg · CARBOHYDRATE 28g · DIETARY FIBER 4g · PROTEIN 6g

BUTTERNUT SQUASH FRIES

½ **teaspoon garlic powder**

¼ **teaspoon salt**

¼ **teaspoon ground red pepper**

1 **butternut squash (about 2½ pounds), peeled, seeded and cut into 2-inch-thin slices**

2 **teaspoons vegetable oil**

1 Combine garlic powder, salt and ground red pepper in small bowl; set aside.

2 Place squash in large bowl. Drizzle with oil and sprinkle with seasoning mix; gently toss to coat.

3 Preheat air fryer to 390°F. Cook in batches 16 to 18 minutes, shaking halfway during cooking, until squash is tender and begins to brown.

MAKES 4 SERVINGS

CALORIES 150 · TOTAL FAT 2.5g · SATURATED FAT 0g · CHOLESTEROL 0mg
SODIUM 160mg · CARBOHYDRATE 33g · DIETARY FIBER 6g · PROTEIN 3g

GRILLED EGGPLANT ROLL-UPS

4 **slices Grilled Eggplant (recipe follows)**

¼ **cup hummus**

¼ **cup crumbled reduced-fat feta cheese**

¼ **cup chopped green onions**

4 **tomato slices, cut in half**

1 Prepare Grilled Eggplant. Spread 1 tablespoon hummus on each eggplant slice. Top with 1 tablespoon feta cheese, 1 tablespoon green onions and 2 tomato halves.

2 Roll up tightly. Serve immediately.

MAKES 2 SERVINGS

GRILLED EGGPLANT: Preheat air fryer to 350°F. Spray basket with nonstick cooking spray. Sprinkle four (1-inch-thick) eggplant slices with ½ teaspoon salt; let stand 15 minutes. Brush eggplant lightly with olive oil. Cook in batches 5 minutes; turn and brush with 1 teaspoon olive oil. Cook 5 minutes or until tender.

CALORIES 160 · TOTAL FAT 8g · SATURATED FAT 3g · CHOLESTEROL 10mg
SODIUM 460mg · CARBOHYDRATE 9g · DIETARY FIBER 2g · PROTEIN 8g

GARLIC AIR-FRIED FRIES

2 large potatoes, peeled and cut into matchstick strips

2 teaspoons plus 1 tablespoon olive oil, divided

1½ teaspoons minced garlic

½ teaspoon dried parsley flakes

½ teaspoon salt

¼ teaspoon ground black pepper

1 Preheat air fryer to 390°F. Line basket with parchment paper.

2 Combine potato strips and 2 teaspoons oil in medium bowl; toss well.

3 Cook in batches 8 to 10 minutes, tossing occasionally, until golden brown and crispy.

4 While fries are cooking, combine remaining 1 tablespoon oil, garlic, parsley flakes, salt and pepper in small bowl.

5 Toss warm fries with garlic sauce. Serve immediately.

MAKES 4 SERVINGS

CALORIES 140 · TOTAL FAT 6g · SATURATED FAT 1g · CHOLESTEROL 0mg
SODIUM 300mg · CARBOHYDRATE 19g · DIETARY FIBER 1g · PROTEIN 2g

ORANGE GLAZED CARROTS

1 **package (32 ounces) baby carrots**

1 **tablespoon packed light brown sugar**

1 **tablespoon orange juice**

1 **tablespoon melted butter**

¼ **teaspoon ground cinnamon**

⅛ **teaspoon ground nutmeg**

Orange peel and fresh chopped parsley (optional)

1 Place carrots in large bowl. Combine brown sugar, orange juice and butter in small bowl. Pour over carrots; toss well.

2 Preheat air fryer to 390°F.

3 Cook 6 to 8 minutes, shaking occasionally during cooking, until carrots are tender and lightly browned. Remove to serving dish. Sprinkle with cinnamon and nutmeg. Garnish with orange peel and parsley.

MAKES 6 SERVINGS

CALORIES 80 · TOTAL FAT 2g · SATURATED FAT 1g · CHOLESTEROL 5mg
SODIUM 120mg · CARBOHYDRATE 15g · DIETARY FIBER 4g · PROTEIN 1g

BITE-YOU-BACK ROASTED EDAMAME

2 teaspoons vegetable oil

2 teaspoons honey

¼ teaspoon wasabi powder*

1 package (about 12 ounces) shelled edamame, thawed if frozen

Kosher salt (optional)

*Wasabi powder can be found in the Asian section of most supermarkets and in Asian specialty markets.

1   Combine oil, honey and wasabi powder in large bowl; mix well. Add edamame; toss to coat.

2   Preheat air fryer to 370°F.

3   Cook 12 to 14 minutes, shaking occasionally during cooking, until lightly browned. Remove from basket to large bowl; sprinkle generously with salt, if desired. Cool completely before serving. Store in airtight container.

MAKES 4 SERVINGS

CALORIES 120 · TOTAL FAT 6g · SATURATED FAT 0g · CHOLESTEROL 0mg
SODIUM 5mg · CARBOHYDRATE 9g · DIETARY FIBER 4g · PROTEIN 10g

EGGPLANT PIZZAS

1 **medium eggplant, sliced into ½-inch rounds**

1 **large egg**

1 **tablespoon water**

¾ **cup seasoned Italian bread crumbs**

½ **cup marinara sauce**

½ **cup (2 ounces) shredded mozzarella cheese**

Chopped fresh basil

1 Preheat air fryer to 370°F. Line basket with foil.

2 Beat egg and water in shallow dish. Place bread crumbs in another shallow dish. Dip eggplant in egg, letting excess drip back into dish. Dredge in bread crumbs, pressing gently to adhere. Spray with nonstick cooking spray.

3 Cook in batches 10 to 12 minutes or until slightly tender and golden brown.

4 Place about 1 tablespoon marinara sauce on top of each eggplant slice. Top with cheese. Return to air fryer 3 to 5 minutes or until cheese is melted and golden brown.

5 Sprinkle with basil.

MAKES 4 SERVINGS

NOTE: Add bell peppers, sliced tomatoes, olives or any other favorite topping.

CALORIES 180 · TOTAL FAT 5g · SATURATED FAT 2g · CHOLESTEROL 55mg
SODIUM 550mg · CARBOHYDRATE 25g · DIETARY FIBER 4g · PROTEIN 10g

ROASTED BUTTERNUT SQUASH

1 pound butternut squash, peeled and cut into 1-inch cubes (about 4 cups)

2 medium onions, coarsely chopped

8 ounces carrots, peeled and cut into ½-inch diagonal slices (about 2 cups)

1 tablespoon packed dark brown sugar

¼ teaspoon salt

Black pepper (optional)

1 Combine vegetables in large bowl. Spray with nonstick cooking spray; toss gently. Sprinkle with brown sugar, salt and pepper, if desired.

2 Preheat air fryer to 390°F. Spray basket with cooking spray.

3 Bake 20 to 25 minutes, shaking occasionally during cooking, until vegetables are tender and brown.

MAKES 5 SERVINGS

CALORIES 80 · TOTAL FAT 0g · SATURATED FAT 0g · CHOLESTEROL 0mg
SODIUM 160mg · CARBOHYDRATE 21g · DIETARY FIBER 4g · PROTEIN 2g

ORANGE AND MAPLE-GLAZED ROASTED BEETS

4 **medium beets, scrubbed**

¼ **cup orange juice**

3 **tablespoons balsamic or cider vinegar**

2 **tablespoons maple syrup**

2 **teaspoons grated orange peel, divided**

1 **teaspoon Dijon mustard**

Salt and black pepper

1 **to 2 tablespoons chopped fresh mint (optional)**

1 Peel and cut beets in half lengthwise; cut into wedges. Place in large bowl.

2 Whisk orange juice, vinegar, maple syrup, 1 teaspoon orange peel and mustard in small bowl until well blended. Pour half over beets.

3 Preheat air fryer to 390°F.

4 Cook 22 to 25 minutes, shaking occasionally during cooking, until softened. Remove to serving dish; pour remaining orange juice mixture over beets. Season with salt and pepper. Sprinkle with remaining 1 teaspoon orange peel and mint, if desired.

MAKES 4 SERVINGS

SERVING SUGGESTION: The flavors of this recipe make it a great side dish to serve at your holiday meal.

CALORIES 80 · TOTAL FAT 0g · SATURATED FAT 0g · CHOLESTEROL 0mg
SODIUM 100mg · CARBOHYDRATE 19g · DIETARY FIBER 2g · PROTEIN 2g

HERBED POTATO CHIPS

1 tablespoon minced fresh dill, thyme or rosemary leaves *or* 1 teaspoon dried dill weed, thyme or rosemary

¼ teaspoon garlic salt

⅛ teaspoon black pepper

2 medium red potatoes

¾ cup sour cream

1 Combine dill, garlic salt and pepper in small bowl; set aside.

2 Cut potatoes crosswise into very thin slices, about ¹⁄₁₆ inch thick. Pat dry with paper towels. Spray potatoes with nonstick cooking spray; sprinkle evenly with seasoning mixture.

3 Preheat air fryer to 390°F. Line basket with parchment paper; spray with cooking spray.

4 Cook 10 to 12 minutes, shaking during cooking and spraying occasionally with cooking spray until golden brown.

5 Cool. Serve with sour cream.

MAKES 2 SERVINGS

CALORIES 150 · TOTAL FAT 0g · SATURATED FAT 0g · CHOLESTEROL 0mg
SODIUM 280mg · CARBOHYDRATE 34g · DIETARY FIBER 4g · PROTEIN 4g

BACON-ROASTED BRUSSELS SPROUTS

1 pound Brussels sprouts

2 slices bacon, cut into ½-inch pieces

2 teaspoons packed brown sugar

Salt and black pepper

1 Trim ends from Brussels sprouts; cut in half lengthwise.

2 Combine Brussels sprouts, bacon and brown sugar in large bowl.

3 Preheat air fryer to 390°F. Cook 15 to 18 minutes, shaking occasionally during cooking, until golden brown. Season with salt and pepper.

MAKES 4 SERVINGS

CALORIES 120 · TOTAL FAT 6g · SATURATED FAT 2g · CHOLESTEROL 10mg
SODIUM 120mg · CARBOHYDRATE 13g · DIETARY FIBER 4g · PROTEIN 6g

POTATO BALLS

2 cups refrigerated leftover mashed potatoes*

2 tablespoons all-purpose flour, plus additional for rolling balls

⅔ cup shredded reduced-fat Cheddar cheese

¼ cup chopped green onions

1 large egg

½ teaspoon salt

¼ teaspoon black pepper

1½ cups seasoned dry bread crumbs

If you don't have leftover potatoes, prepare 2 cups instant mashed potatoes and refrigerate at least 1 hour.

1 Combine potatoes, 2 tablespoons flour, cheese and green onions in large bowl. Scoop out about 2 tablespoons mixture and roll into a 1-inch ball, adding additional flour, if necessary, making about 20 balls.

2 Beat egg, salt and pepper in medium bowl. Place bread crumbs in shallow dish. Dip balls in egg, letting excess drip back into bowl, then in bread crumbs until fully coated. Place on baking sheet; refrigerate 30 minutes.

3 Preheat air fryer to 390°F. Spray basket with nonstick cooking spray.

4 Cook in batches 8 to 10 minutes or until balls are browned and heated through.

MAKES 20 BALLS

CALORIES 70 · TOTAL FAT 1.5g · SATURATED FAT 0.5g · CHOLESTEROL 10mg
SODIUM 270mg · CARBOHYDRATE 12g · DIETARY FIBER 0g · PROTEIN 3g

SAVORY STUFFED TOMATOES

2 large ripe tomatoes (1 to 1¼ pounds total)

¾ cup garlic- or Caesar-flavored croutons

¼ cup chopped pitted kalamata olives (optional)

2 tablespoons chopped fresh basil

1 clove garlic, minced

2 tablespoons grated Parmesan or Romano cheese

1 tablespoon olive oil

1 Cut tomatoes in half crosswise; discard seeds. Scrape out and reserve pulp. Set aside tomato shells.

2 Chop up tomato pulp; place in medium bowl. Add croutons, olives, if desired, basil and garlic; toss well. Spoon mixture into tomato shells. Sprinkle with Parmesan cheese; drizzle oil over shells.

3 Preheat air fryer to 350°F. Line basket with foil or parchment paper.

4 Cook 5 to 7 minutes or until heated through.

MAKES 4 SERVINGS

CALORIES 100 · TOTAL FAT 7g · SATURATED FAT 2g · CHOLESTEROL 5mg
SODIUM 270mg · CARBOHYDRATE 8g · DIETARY FIBER 1g · PROTEIN 3g

ROASTED CURRIED CAULIFLOWER AND BRUSSELS SPROUTS

2 **pounds cauliflower florets**

12 **ounces Brussels sprouts, cleaned and cut in half lengthwise**

⅓ **cup olive oil**

½ **teaspoon sea salt**

½ **teaspoon black pepper**

2½ **tablespoons curry powder**

½ **cup chopped fresh cilantro**

1   Preheat air fryer to 370°F. Line basket with foil.

2   Combine cauliflower, Brussels sprouts and oil in large bowl; toss to coat.

3   Sprinkle with salt, pepper and curry powder; toss to coat.

4   Cook in batches 12 to 15 minutes or until golden brown, shaking halfway through cooking.

5   Add cilantro; toss until blended.

MAKES 10 SERVINGS

CALORIES 110 · TOTAL FAT 8g · SATURATED FAT 1g · CHOLESTEROL 0mg
SODIUM 135mg · CARBOHYDRATE 9g · DIETARY FIBER 4g · PROTEIN 3g

CAPRESE PORTOBELLOS

2 tablespoons butter

½ teaspoon minced garlic

1 teaspoon dried parsley flakes

4 portobello mushrooms, stems removed

1 cup (4 ounces) shredded part-skim mozzarella cheese

1 cup cherry or grape tomatoes, thinly sliced

2 tablespoons fresh basil, thinly sliced

Balsamic glaze

1 Combine butter, garlic and parsley flakes in small microwavable dish. Microwave on LOW (30%) 30 seconds or until melted.

2 Wash mushrooms thoroughly; dry on paper towels. Brush both sides of mushrooms with butter mixture.

3 Preheat air fryer to 390°F. Spray basket with nonstick cooking spray.

4 Fill mushroom caps with about ¼ cup cheese each. Top with sliced tomatoes. Cook 5 to 7 minutes or until cheese is melted and lightly browned. Top with basil.

5 Drizzle with balsamic glaze before serving.

MAKES 4 SERVINGS

CALORIES 160 · TOTAL FAT 12g · SATURATED FAT 7g · CHOLESTEROL 35mg
SODIUM 200mg · CARBOHYDRATE 6g · DIETARY FIBER 2g · PROTEIN 9g

AIR-FRIED CAULIFLOWER FLORETS

1 **head cauliflower**

1 **tablespoon olive oil**

3 **tablespoons grated Parmesan cheese**

2 **tablespoons panko bread crumbs**

½ **teaspoon salt**

½ **teaspoon chopped fresh parsley**

¼ **teaspoon ground black pepper**

1 Cut cauliflower into florets. Place in large bowl. Drizzle with oil. Sprinkle Parmesan cheese, panko, salt, parsley and pepper over cauliflower; toss to coat.

2 Preheat air fryer to 390°F. Spray basket with nonstick cooking spray.

3 Cook in batches 18 to 20 minutes or until browned, shaking every 6 minutes during cooking.

MAKES 4 SERVINGS

CALORIES 100 · TOTAL FAT 5g · SATURATED FAT 1.5g · CHOLESTEROL 0mg
SODIUM 430mg · CARBOHYDRATE 9g · DIETARY FIBER 3g · PROTEIN 5g

ITALIAN-STYLE ROASTED VEGETABLES

1 **small eggplant, cut into chunks**

1 **small zucchini, cut into chunks**

1 **small red bell pepper, cut into chunks**

1 **small yellow bell pepper, cut into chunks**

1 **small onion, cut into chunks**

1 **teaspoon minced garlic**

½ **teaspoon salt**

¼ **teaspoon red pepper flakes**

½ **teaspoon dried basil**

½ **teaspoon dried oregano**

1 **tablespoon olive oil**

1 **teaspoon vinegar**

Grated Parmesan cheese (optional)

1 Combine vegetables in large bowl. Toss with garlic, salt, red pepper flakes, basil, oregano, oil and vinegar.

2 Preheat air fryer to 390°F. Spray basket with nonstick cooking spray.

3 Cook in batches 12 to 15 minutes, shaking halfway during cooking until vegetables are tender and browned.

4 Sprinkle with Parmesan cheese before serving, if desired.

MAKES 6 SERVINGS

CALORIES 70 · TOTAL FAT 2.5g · SATURATED FAT 0g · CHOLESTEROL 0mg
SODIUM 200mg · CARBOHYDRATE 11g · DIETARY FIBER 3g · PROTEIN 2g

CAPRESE STUFFED ZUCCHINI BOATS

3 medium zucchini

1 package (3 ounces) ramen noodles, any flavor, broken into small pieces*

1 tomato, finely chopped

½ cup (2 ounces) shredded part-skim mozzarella cheese

2 tablespoons fresh chopped basil

1 tablespoon olive oil

1 clove garlic, minced

½ teaspoon salt

Discard seasoning packet.

1 Slice zucchini in half lengthwise; scoop out seeds, leaving the shell. Cut off ends of zucchini or trim to fit in air fryer basket.

2 Cook ramen noodles in boiling water 2 minutes; drain and place in large bowl. Add tomato, cheese, basil, oil, garlic and salt; stir to combine. Divide mixture among shells.

3 Preheat air fryer to 350°F. Cook in batches 15 to 20 minutes or until zucchini is tender and noodles are lightly browned.

MAKES 6 SERVINGS

CALORIES 130 · TOTAL FAT 7g · SATURATED FAT 2.5g · CHOLESTEROL 5mg
SODIUM 530mg · CARBOHYDRATE 13g · DIETARY FIBER 1g · PROTEIN 5g

CRISPY FRIES WITH HERBED DIPPING SAUCE

Herbed Dipping Sauce (recipe follows)

2 **large unpeeled baking potatoes**

1 **tablespoon vegetable oil**

½ **teaspoon kosher salt**

1 Prepare Herbed Dipping Sauce; set aside.

2 Cut potatoes into ¼-inch strips. Toss potato strips with oil in large bowl to coat evenly.

3 Preheat air fryer to 390°F. Spray basket with nonstick cooking spray.

4 Cook in batches 18 to 20 minutes, shaking occasionally during cooking, until golden brown and crispy. Sprinkle with salt. Serve immediately with Herbed Dipping Sauce.

MAKES 3 SERVINGS

HERBED DIPPING SAUCE: Stir ¼ cup mayonnaise, 1 tablespoon chopped fresh herbs (such as basil, parsley, oregano and/or dill), ¼ teaspoon salt and ⅛ teaspoon black pepper in small bowl until smooth and well blended. Cover and refrigerate until ready to serve.

CALORIES 290 · TOTAL FAT 12g · SATURATED FAT 1.5g · CHOLESTEROL 5mg
SODIUM 660mg · CARBOHYDRATE 44g · DIETARY FIBER 4g · PROTEIN 4g

STUFFED PORTOBELLOS

1 teaspoon olive oil

½ cup diced red bell pepper

½ cup diced onion

¼ teaspoon dried thyme

⅔ cup panko bread crumbs

⅔ cup diced tomatoes

¼ cup grated Parmesan cheese

¼ cup chopped fresh parsley

4 portobello mushroom caps

1 Heat oil in medium nonstick skillet over medium-high heat. Add bell pepper and onion; cook and stir 5 minutes or until tender and lightly browned. Season with thyme.

2 Combine vegetable mixture, panko, tomatoes, Parmesan cheese and parsley in medium bowl. Mound vegetable mixture into mushrooms.

3 Preheat air fryer to 390°F. Spray basket with nonstick cooking spray.

4 Cook 5 to 7 minutes or until mushrooms are tender and topping is lightly browned.

MAKES 4 SERVINGS

ALTERNATE COOKING METHOD: Toss oil and vegetables in baking dish that fits inside air fryer. Place dish in air fryer basket; cook 3 to 5 minutes or until vegetables are tender. Proceed with step 2.

CALORIES 130 · TOTAL FAT 4g · SATURATED FAT 1.5g · CHOLESTEROL 5mg
SODIUM 150mg · CARBOHYDRATE 18g · DIETARY FIBER 2g · PROTEIN 7g

SNACKS & GOODIES

KALE CHIPS

- **1 large bunch kale (about 1 pound)**
- **1 tablespoon olive oil**
- **1 teaspoon garlic powder**
- **½ teaspoon salt**
- **½ teaspoon black pepper**

1 Wash kale and pat dry with paper towels. Remove center ribs and stems; discard. Cut leaves into 2- to 3-inch-wide pieces.

2 Combine leaves, oil, garlic powder, salt and pepper in large bowl; toss to coat.

3 Preheat air fryer to 390°F.

4 Cook in batches 3 to 4 minutes or until edges are lightly browned and leaves are crisp. Cool completely. Store in airtight container.

MAKES 6 SERVINGS

CALORIES 60 · TOTAL FAT 3g · SATURATED FAT 0g · CHOLESTEROL 0mg
SODIUM 230mg · CARBOHYDRATE 7g · DIETARY FIBER 3g · PROTEIN 3g

BEET CHIPS

3 medium beets (red and/or golden), trimmed

1½ tablespoons extra virgin olive oil

¼ teaspoon salt

¼ teaspoon black pepper

1 Cut beets into very thin slices, about ⅛ inch thick. Combine beets, oil, salt and pepper in medium bowl; gently toss to coat.

2 Preheat air fryer to 390°F.

3 Cook 15 to 18 minutes, shaking occasionally during cooking, until darkened and crisp. Cool completely.

MAKES 3 SERVINGS

CALORIES 100 · TOTAL FAT 7g · SATURATED FAT 1g · CHOLESTEROL 0mg
SODIUM 260mg · CARBOHYDRATE 8g · DIETARY FIBER 2g · PROTEIN 1g

EVERYTHING SEASONING DIP WITH BAGEL CHIPS

- **2 large bagels, sliced vertically into rounds**
- **1 container (12 ounces) whipped cream cheese**
- **1½ tablespoons green onion tops, chopped**
- **1 teaspoon minced onion**
- **1 teaspoon minced garlic**
- **1 teaspoon sesame seeds**
- **1 teaspoon poppy seeds**
- **¼ teaspoon kosher salt**

1. Preheat air fryer to 350°F.

2. Coat bagel rounds generously with butter-flavored nonstick cooking spray. Cook 7 to 8 minutes, shaking occasionally, until golden brown.

3. Combine cream cheese, green onions, minced onion, garlic, sesame seeds, poppy seeds and salt in medium bowl; stir to blend.

4. Serve chips with dip.

MAKES ABOUT 2 CUPS DIP (ABOUT 16 SERVINGS)

CALORIES 110 · TOTAL FAT 8g · SATURATED FAT 4.5g · CHOLESTEROL 20mg
SODIUM 170mg · CARBOHYDRATE 8g · DIETARY FIBER 0g · PROTEIN 3g

SAVORY ZUCCHINI STIX

- **3 tablespoons seasoned dry bread crumbs**
- **2 tablespoons grated Parmesan cheese**
- **1 egg white**
- **1 teaspoon reduced-fat (2%) milk**
- **2 small zucchini (about 4 ounces each), cut lengthwise into quarters**
- **⅓ cup pasta sauce, warmed**

1 Combine bread crumbs and Parmesan cheese in shallow dish. Combine egg white and milk in another shallow dish; beat with fork until well blended.

2 Dip each zucchini wedge into crumb mixture, then into egg white mixture, letting excess drip back into dish. Roll again in crumb mixture to coat. Spray zucchini with nonstick cooking spray.

3 Preheat air fryer to 370°F. Spray basket with cooking spray.

4 Cook 8 to 10 minutes, shaking halfway during cooking, until golden brown. Serve with pasta sauce.

MAKES 4 SERVINGS

CALORIES 60 · TOTAL FAT 2g · SATURATED FAT 1g · CHOLESTEROL 5mg
SODIUM 180mg · CARBOHYDRATE 8g · DIETARY FIBER 1g · PROTEIN 4g

ROASTED CHICKPEAS

1 **can (about 15 ounces) chickpeas, rinsed and drained**

1 **tablespoon olive oil**

¼ **teaspoon salt**

¼ **teaspoon black pepper**

¼ **tablespoon chili powder**

¼ **teaspoon ground red pepper**

1 **lime, cut into wedges (optional)**

1 Combine chickpeas, oil, salt and black pepper in large bowl; toss to mix well.

2 Preheat air fryer to 390°F.

3 Cook 8 to 10 minutes, shaking occasionally during cooking, until chickpeas begin to brown.

4 Sprinkle with chili powder and ground red pepper. Serve with lime wedges, if desired.

MAKES 1 CUP (4 SERVINGS)

NOTE: Top salads with chickpeas for a delicious crunch and healthier alternative to croutons.

CALORIES 120 · TOTAL FAT 4.5g · SATURATED FAT 0g · CHOLESTEROL 0mg
SODIUM 390mg · CARBOHYDRATE 15g · DIETARY FIBER 4g · PROTEIN 4g

SAVORY PITA CHIPS

- **2 whole wheat or white pita bread rounds**
- **2 tablespoons grated Parmesan cheese**
- **1 teaspoon dried basil**
- **¼ teaspoon garlic powder**

1 Carefully cut each pita round in half horizontally; split into two rounds. Cut each round into six wedges. Spray wedges with nonstick cooking spray.

2 Combine Parmesan cheese, basil and garlic powder in small bowl; sprinkle evenly over pita wedges.

3 Preheat air fryer to 350°F.

4 Cook 8 to 10 minutes, shaking occasionally during cooking, until golden brown. Cool completely.

MAKES 4 SERVINGS

CINNAMON CRISPS: Substitute cooking spray for olive oil cooking spray and 1 tablespoon sugar mixed with ¼ teaspoon ground cinnamon for Parmesan cheese, basil and garlic powder.

CALORIES 100 · TOTAL FAT 1.5g · SATURATED FAT 1g · CHOLESTEROL 5mg
SODIUM 230mg · CARBOHYDRATE 18g · DIETARY FIBER 0g · PROTEIN 5g

EGGPLANT NIBBLES

1 **egg**

1 **tablespoon water**

½ **cup seasoned dry bread crumbs**

1 **Asian eggplant or 1 small globe eggplant**

Marinara sauce (optional)

1 Beat egg and water in shallow dish. Place bread crumbs in another shallow dish.

2 Cut ends off of eggplant. Cut into sticks about 3 inches long by ½-inch wide.

3 Coat eggplant sticks in egg, letting excess drip back into dish, then roll in bread crumbs. Spray with olive oil cooking spray.

4 Preheat air fryer to 370°F. Line basket with foil or parchment paper.

5 Cook 12 to 14 minutes, shaking occasionally during cooking, until eggplant is tender and lightly browned. Serve with marinara sauce, if desired.

MAKES 4 SERVINGS

CALORIES 100 · TOTAL FAT 2g · SATURATED FAT 0.5g · CHOLESTEROL 45mg
SODIUM 220mg · CARBOHYDRATE 17g · DIETARY FIBER 3g · PROTEIN 5g

SPICY BAKED SWEET POTATO CHIPS

- **1 teaspoon sugar**
- **½ teaspoon smoked paprika**
- **¼ teaspoon salt**
- **¼ teaspoon ground red pepper**
- **2 medium sweet potatoes, unpeeled and cut into very thin slices**
- **2 teaspoons vegetable oil**

1. Combine sugar, paprika, salt and ground red pepper in small bowl; set aside.

2. Place potatoes in large bowl. Drizzle with oil; toss to coat. Sprinkle with seasoning mix.

3. Preheat air fryer to 390°F. Cook in batches 15 to 18 minutes, shaking occasionally until chips are lightly browned and crisp. Cool completely.

MAKES 4 SERVINGS

CALORIES 80 · TOTAL FAT 2.5g · SATURATED FAT 0g · CHOLESTEROL 0mg
SODIUM 180mg · CARBOHYDRATE 13g · DIETARY FIBER 2g · PROTEIN 1g

CORN TORTILLA CHIPS

**6 (6-inch) corn tortillas,
  preferably day-old**

½ **teaspoon salt**

Salsa or guacamole (optional)

1 If tortillas are fresh, let stand, uncovered, in single layer on wire rack 1 to 2 hours to dry slightly.

2 Stack tortillas; cut tortillas into 6 equal wedges. Spray tortillas generously with nonstick olive oil cooking spray.

3 Preheat air fryer to 370°F.

4 Cook in batches 5 to 6 minutes, shaking halfway through cooking. Sprinkle with salt. Serve with salsa or guacamole, if desired.

**MAKES 3 DOZEN CHIPS
(12 SERVINGS)**

NOTE: Tortilla chips are served with salsa as a snack, used as the base for nachos and used as scoops for guacamole, other dips or refried beans. They are best eaten fresh, but can be stored, tightly covered, in a cool place 2 or 3 days.

CALORIES 30 · TOTAL FAT 0g · SATURATED FAT 0g · CHOLESTEROL 0mg
SODIUM 100mg · CARBOHYDRATE 6g · DIETARY FIBER 0g · PROTEIN 1g

SWEETS & DESSERTS

APPLE FRIES WITH CARAMEL SAUCE

½ **cup all-purpose flour**

2 **large eggs**

1 **cup crushed graham cracker crumbs *or* 4 large graham crackers, finely crushed**

¼ **cup granulated sugar**

2 **medium Gala apples, cored and cut into 8 wedges each**

CARAMEL SAUCE

½ **cup packed brown sugar**

¼ **cup whipping cream**

2 **tablespoons butter**

2 **tablespoons corn syrup**

¼ **teaspoon salt**

1 Place flour in small bowl. Beat eggs in shallow dish. Combine cracker crumbs with granulated sugar in another shallow dish.

2 Preheat air fryer to 390°F. Line basket with parchment paper.

3 Coat apple wedges in flour then in eggs, letting excess drip back into bowl. Coat with cracker crumb mixture; place on plate. Refrigerate 15 to 30 minutes.

4 Preheat air fryer to 390°F. Line basket with parchment paper. Cook apples 6 to 8 minutes until slightly tender and golden brown.

5 Prepare Caramel Sauce. Combine brown sugar, cream, butter, corn syrup and salt in small saucepan. Heat over medium-low heat until warmed.

6 Serve apple fries with Caramel Sauce.

MAKES 4 SERVINGS

CALORIES 320 • TOTAL FAT 11g • SATURATED FAT 6g • CHOLESTEROL 85mg
SODIUM 210mg • CARBOHYDRATE 52g • DIETARY FIBER 2g • PROTEIN 5g

SAUTÉED APPLES SUPREME

2 **small Granny Smith apples** *or* **1 large Granny Smith apple**

1 **teaspoon butter, melted**

2 **tablespoons unsweetened apple juice or cider**

1 **teaspoon packed brown sugar**

½ **teaspoon ground cinnamon**

⅔ **cup vanilla ice cream or frozen yogurt (optional)**

2 **tablespoons chopped walnuts, toasted***

*To toast nuts, cook in preheated 325°F parchment-lined air fryer 3 to 4 minutes or until golden brown.

1 Cut apples into quarters; remove cores and cut into ½-inch-thick slices. Toss butter and apples in medium bowl.

2 Combine apple juice, brown sugar and cinnamon in small bowl; toss with apples.

3 Preheat air fryer to 350°F. Line basket with parchment paper; spray with nonstick cooking spray.

4 Cook 6 to 8 minutes, shaking halfway through cooking, until soft and lightly golden. Transfer to serving bowls; serve with ice cream, if desired. Sprinkle with walnuts.

MAKES 2 SERVINGS

CALORIES 170 · TOTAL FAT 7g · SATURATED FAT 1.5g · CHOLESTEROL 5mg
SODIUM 0mg · CARBOHYDRATE 25g · DIETARY FIBER 5g · PROTEIN 2g

SHORTBREAD COOKIE STICKS

1¼ **cups all-purpose flour**

3 **tablespoons sugar**

½ **cup (1 stick) butter**

½ **cup chocolate chips**

1 **tablespoon whipping cream**

¼ **cup sprinkles**

1 Combine flour and sugar in large bowl; cut in butter with pastry cutter until fine crumbs form. Using damp hands, form dough into a ball and knead until smooth.

2 Roll dough to ½-inch thickness on lightly floured work surface. Cut into ½-inch×4-inch sticks.

3 Preheat air fryer to 350°F.

4 Cook sticks in batches 5 to 7 minutes or until lightly browned. Remove from basket; cool completely.

5 Combine chocolate chips and cream in small bowl. Cover and microwave 30 seconds or until melted; stir. Drizzle sticks with chocolate. Top with sprinkles. Place on plate or cookie sheet. Refrigerate until chocolate is set.

MAKES 1½ DOZEN STICKS

CALORIES 120 · TOTAL FAT 8g · SATURATED FAT 4g · CHOLESTEROL 15mg
SODIUM 0mg · CARBOHYDRATE 14g · DIETARY FIBER 1g · PROTEIN 1g

PEACHES WITH RASPBERRY SAUCE

1 **package (10 ounces) frozen raspberries, thawed**

1½ **teaspoons lemon juice**

2 **tablespoons packed brown sugar**

½ **teaspoon ground cinnamon**

1 **can (15 ounces) peach halves in juice (4 halves)**

Foil

2 **teaspoons butter, cut into small pieces**

Fresh mint sprigs (optional)

1 Combine raspberries and lemon juice in food processor fitted with metal blade; process until smooth. Refrigerate until ready to serve.

2 Preheat air fryer to 350°F.

3 Combine brown sugar and cinnamon in medium bowl; coat peach halves with mixture. Place peach halves, cut sides up, on foil. Dot with butter. Fold foil over peaches. Place packet in basket.

4 Cook 6 to 8 minutes or until peaches are soft and lightly browned.

5 To serve, spoon 2 tablespoons raspberry sauce over each peach half. Garnish with mint.

MAKES 4 SERVINGS

CALORIES 120 · TOTAL FAT 2g · SATURATED FAT 1g · CHOLESTEROL 5mg
SODIUM 5mg · CARBOHYDRATE 28g · DIETARY FIBER 5g · PROTEIN 1g

HASSELBACK APPLES

2 **medium apples, unpeeled**
 Foil
2 **tablespoons packed brown sugar**
2 **tablespoons finely chopped walnuts**
½ **teaspoon ground cinnamon**
2 **tablespoons butter, melted**
½ **cup vanilla ice cream (optional)**

1 Cut apples in half vertically. Scoop out seeds. Lay flat side down; cut slits ⅛ inch apart almost all the way down. Place apples on foil; wrapping lightly up sides of apple.

2 Combine brown sugar, walnuts and cinnamon in small bowl. Brush butter over tops of apples, letting drip inside slits. Sprinkle apples with brown sugar mixture.

3 Preheat air fryer to 350°F. Place foil-wrapped apples in basket. Cook 12 to 15 minutes or until apples are softened and browned.

4 Serve with ice cream, if desired.

MAKES 4 SERVINGS

NOTE: If apples brown too quickly on top, brush with additional melted butter.

CALORIES 150 · TOTAL FAT 8g · SATURATED FAT 4g · CHOLESTEROL 15mg
SODIUM 0mg · CARBOHYDRATE 20g · DIETARY FIBER 2g · PROTEIN 1g

APRICOT TARTLETS

4 sheets frozen phyllo dough, thawed

1 can (15 ounces) apricot halves in juice (not in syrup), drained

4 tablespoons apricot preserves

1 tablespoon powdered sugar

1 teaspoon ground cinnamon

1   Place one sheet of phyllo dough on lightly-floured work surface; keep remaining sheets covered with plastic wrap and damp towel. Spray phyllo dough with nonstick cooking spray. Fold in half to create 8×6-inch rectangle; spray with cooking spray.

2   Place 3 apricot halves, cut side up, in center of phyllo dough. Spread 1 tablespoon preserves over apricots. Fold and pleat about 1 inch of dough around edges to form round tartlet shell. Repeat with remaining ingredients to form 3 more tartlets.

3   Preheat air fryer to 350°F. Line basket with foil; spray with cooking spray.

4   Cook 6 to 8 minutes or until golden brown and crisp. Combine powdered sugar and cinnamon in small bowl; sprinkle over tartlets. Serve warm.

**MAKES 4 SERVINGS
(1 TARTLET PER SERVING)**

TIP: Phyllo dough dries out very quickly and crumbles easily. Keep thawed phyllo dough wrapped or covered until all the ingredients are assembled and you are ready to work with the dough.

CALORIES 190 · TOTAL FAT 1g · SATURATED FAT 0g · CHOLESTEROL 0mg
SODIUM 95mg · CARBOHYDRATE 44g · DIETARY FIBER 2g · PROTEIN 2g

PLUM-GINGER BRUSCHETTA

1 **sheet frozen puff pastry (half of 17¼-ounce package), thawed**

2 **cups chopped unpeeled firm ripe plums (about 3 medium)**

2 **tablespoons sugar**

2 **tablespoons chopped candied ginger**

1 **tablespoon all-purpose flour**

2 **teaspoons lemon juice**

⅛ **teaspoon ground cinnamon**

2 **tablespoons apple jelly *or* apricot preserves**

1 Cut puff pastry sheet lengthwise into three strips. Cut each strip crosswise in thirds to make nine pieces.

2 Preheat air fryer to 370°F. Line basket with parchment paper. Cook in batches 5 to 6 minutes or until puffed and lightly browned.

3 Meanwhile, combine plums, sugar, ginger, flour, lemon juice and cinnamon in medium bowl.

4 Gently brush each puff pastry piece with about ½ teaspoon jelly; top with scant ¼ cup plum mixture. Cook in batches 1 to 2 minutes or until fruit is tender.

MAKES 9 SERVINGS

CALORIES 60 · TOTAL FAT 1.5g · SATURATED FAT 0g · CHOLESTEROL 0mg
SODIUM 20mg · CARBOHYDRATE 11g · DIETARY FIBER 0g · PROTEIN 1g

TROPICAL PINEAPPLE RINGS

1 **can (20 ounces) pineapple slices in pineapple juice**

1 **teaspoon coconut extract**

2 **eggs**

½ **cup all-purpose flour**

1 **cup unsweetened shredded coconut**

1 **cup panko bread crumbs**

Powdered sugar, marachino cherries (optional)

1 Drain pineapple slices, reserving juice. Place pineapple in large resealable food storage bag; add ¼ cup reserved pineapple juice and coconut extract. Refrigerate at least 15 minutes.

2 Whisk eggs and remaining ½ cup pineapple juice in medium bowl.

3 Place flour in shallow dish. Combine coconut and panko in another shallow dish.

4 Remove pineapple from refrigerator; drain juice. Pat slices dry with paper towels.

5 Coat pineapple with flour. Dip in egg mixture, letting excess drip back into bowl, then coat with coconut-panko mixture. Set pineapple on baking sheet. Refrigerate 15 minutes.

6 Preheat air fryer to 350°F. Spray basket with nonstick cooking spray.

7 Cook in batches 5 to 6 minutes or until coating is lightly browned and toasted. Serve warm. Sprinkle with powdered sugar and top with cherries, if desired.

MAKES 10 SERVINGS

CALORIES 150 · TOTAL FAT 4.5g · SATURATED FAT 3.5g · CHOLESTEROL 35mg
SODIUM 50mg · CARBOHYDRATE 24g · DIETARY FIBER 1g · PROTEIN 3g

BAKED PEARS

 1 **tablespoon sugar**

 ¼ **teaspoon ground cinnamon**

 2 **medium ripe Bosc pears, halved lengthwise and cored**

 2 **teaspoons butter**

 ½ **cup pear juice, divided**

 3 **gingersnap cookies, crushed**

1 Combine sugar and cinnamon in small bowl; sprinkle over pear halves. Put ½ teaspoon butter in each pear cavity. Drizzle 1 tablespoon juice over top of each pear.

2 Preheat air fryer to 370°F. Spray basket with nonstick cooking spray. Place pear halves, cut sides up, in basket.

3 Cook 12 to 14 minutes or until pears are browned. Sprinkle with crushed gingersnaps; cook 3 to 4 minutes. Drizzle remaining ¼ cup juice over pears to serve.

MAKES 4 SERVINGS

CALORIES 200 · TOTAL FAT 4g · SATURATED FAT 1.5g · CHOLESTEROL 5mg
SODIUM 115mg · CARBOHYDRATE 40g · DIETARY FIBER 3g · PROTEIN 2g

GINGER BAKED BANANAS WITH CINNAMON CREAM

BAKED BANANAS

- **2 firm ripe bananas, peeled**
- **2 tablespoons butter, melted and divided**
- **1½ teaspoons lemon juice**
- **2 tablespoons packed light brown sugar**
- **2 tablespoons old-fashioned or quick oats**
- **2 tablespoons chopped pecans or walnuts**
- **1½ teaspoons finely chopped crystallized ginger**

CINNAMON CREAM

- **1 teaspoon granulated sugar**
- **½ teaspoon ground cinnamon**
- **½ cup cold whipping cream**

1. Preheat air fryer to 370°F. Place bananas in single layer on parchment paper.

2. Combine 1 tablespoon butter and lemon juice in small bowl; drizzle evenly over bananas.

3. Combine brown sugar, oats, pecans, ginger and remaining 1 tablespoon butter in small bowl; sprinkle evenly over bananas. Cook 5 to 8 minutes or until bananas are hot and topping is bubbly.

4. To prepare Cinnamon Cream, combine granulated sugar and cinnamon in small bowl. Pour cold cream into medium bowl; beat with electric mixer at high speed until soft peaks form. Gradually beat sugar mixture into whipped cream until stiff peaks form.

5. Serve bananas warm with Cinnamon Cream.

MAKES 2 SERVINGS

CALORIES 250 · TOTAL FAT 9g · SATURATED FAT 4g · CHOLESTEROL 15mg
SODIUM 5mg · CARBOHYDRATE 45g · DIETARY FIBER 4g · PROTEIN 2g

INDEX

METRIC CONVERSION CHART

VOLUME MEASUREMENTS (dry)

⅛ teaspoon = 0.5 mL
¼ teaspoon = 1 mL
½ teaspoon = 2 mL
¾ teaspoon = 4 mL
1 teaspoon = 5 mL
1 tablespoon = 15 mL
2 tablespoons = 30 mL
¼ cup = 60 mL
⅓ cup = 75 mL
½ cup = 125 mL
⅔ cup = 150 mL
¾ cup = 175 mL
1 cup = 250 mL
2 cups = 1 pint = 500 mL
3 cups = 750 mL
4 cups = 1 quart = 1 L

VOLUME MEASUREMENTS (fluid)

1 fluid ounce (2 tablespoons) = 30 mL
4 fluid ounces (½ cup) = 125 mL
8 fluid ounces (1 cup) = 250 mL
12 fluid ounces (1½ cups) = 375 mL
16 fluid ounces (2 cups) = 500 mL

WEIGHTS (mass)

½ ounce = 15 g
1 ounce = 30 g
3 ounces = 90 g
4 ounces = 120 g
8 ounces = 225 g
10 ounces = 285 g
12 ounces = 360 g
16 ounces = 1 pound = 450 g

DIMENSIONS

1/16 inch = 2 mm
⅛ inch = 3 mm
¼ inch = 6 mm
½ inch = 1.5 cm
¾ inch = 2 cm
1 inch = 2.5 cm

OVEN TEMPERATURES

250°F = 120°C
275°F = 140°C
300°F = 150°C
325°F = 160°C
350°F = 180°C
375°F = 190°C
400°F = 200°C
425°F = 220°C
450°F = 230°C

BAKING PAN SIZES

Utensil	Size in Inches/Quarts	Metric Volume	Size in Centimeters
Baking or Cake Pan (square or rectangular)	8×8×2	2 L	20×20×5
	9×9×2	2.5 L	23×23×5
	12×8×2	3 L	30×20×5
	13×9×2	3.5 L	33×23×5
Loaf Pan	8×4×3	1.5 L	20×10×7
	9×5×3	2 L	23×13×7
Round Layer Cake Pan	8×1½	1.2 L	20×4
	9×1½	1.5 L	23×4
Pie Plate	8×1¼	750 mL	20×3
	9×1¼	1 L	23×3
Baking Dish or Casserole	1 quart	1 L	—
	1½ quart	1.5 L	—
	2 quart	2 L	—